SHAMANISM:
The Spirit World
of Korea

Studies in Korean Religions and Culture

General Editors:
Lewis R. Lancaster
Chai-shin Yu

SHAMANISM:
The Spirit World
of Korea

edited by
Richard W.I. Guisso
and
Chai-shin Yu

ASIAN HUMANITIES PRESS
Berkeley, California

ASIAN HUMANITIES PRESS

Asian Humanities Press offers to the specialist and the general reader alike the best in new translations of major works and significant original contributions to enhance our understanding of Asian religions, cultures and thought.

1988

Asian Humanities Press
Berkeley, California

ISBN 0-89581-875-2
Library of Congress Catalog Card Number 87-71271

Contents

Acknowledgments

Several persons were instrumental in the production of this volume. We should like, in the first instance, to thank our contributors and the graduate students who provided the preliminary translations from the Korean.

Dr. Kim Inhoe is currently a professor of Ehwa Women's University and the author of *Korean Culture and Education* (Seoul, 1974) as well as numerous articles on shamanism. His article translated here appeared originally in his volume, *Han Kuk Musok ŭi Chong hab jŏk Yŏngu* (Seoul, 1982), pp. 3-29, and the preliminary translation was done by Mr. Yoo Yongsik of the Graduate Centre for Religious Studies at the University of Toronto. Mr. Yoo also drafted a first translation of the two articles by Dr. Chang Chu-kun. Dr. Chang aof Kyunggi University is the author of *Korean Myth* (Seoul, 1961) and *Korean Folk Faith* (Tokyo, 1973) among many other studies of Korean religion. His second article here appeared originally as *Hikak Kodai Nihon To Kankok Bunka(ue)* (Tokyo, 1975), pp. 257-296.

The late Dr. Hahm Pyong-choon was a professor at Yonsei University and a former ambassador to the United States. He is the author of *The Korean Political Tradition and Korean Law* (Seoul, 1967) as well as numerous other studies on Korean civilization. The present article appeared in *Korean Culture*, I:4, pp. 3-10 and II:1, pp. 17-25. Dr. Yu Chai-shin of the Department of East Asian Studies is the author of *Korean and Asian Religious Traditions* (Toronto, 1977), *Early Buddhism and Christianity* (Motilal Banarsidass, 1981), and *Korean Folk Tales* (Toronto, 1983).

Dr. Kim Taegon of Kyunghi University is the author of *An Anthology of Korean Shaman Songs* and *A Collection of Shaman Chants* among other studies. His article appeared originally in *Han Kuk Musok ŭi Chong hab jŏk Yŏngu* (Seoul, 1982), pp. 33-55, and the draft translation was done by Lee Yujin of the Department of Political Science

8

at the University of Toronto. Dr. Kim Kwang-il of Kyunghi University is the author of several studies on the psychiatric aspects of folk-religion and the present article is taken from *Munhoa Mryuhak*, Vol. 5 (1972), pp. 79-106. The draft translation was done by Suh Kikon of Northpark Theological Seminary and Im Hye-young of the University of Toronto. Dr. Lee Du-hyun of Seoul National University, is the author of *Korean Mask Dances* (Seoul, 1969), and *A History of Korean Drama* (Seoul, 1973), and has published widely on the performance aspects of shamanistic ritual. His article was presented as a paper for the International Symposium on Theatre and Ritual, held by the Wenner-Gren Foundation for the Anthropological Research at the Asia Society, New York in August, 1982.

We would also like to acknowledge with gratitude the financial support of Mr. Suh Kikon and the assistance of Ms. Sylvia Waterman and Mrs. Ena Yu in the preparation of the manuscript.

Richard W. L. Guisso

Preface

═══

This collection of essays is the first in a projected series designed to explore selected facets of Korean religion. The idea for the series came about, as do many scholarly projects, when a number of persons, primarily students and teachers, recognized that far too little was known of the subject. As Korea, divided though it is, comes to play a growing role in world affairs, and as Korean Studies become more and more a part of the curriculum at universities and colleges in the West, the need for knowledge of its civilization becomes more urgent. East Asian specialists in the West have long focused their attention primarily on China and Japan, and even though Korean Studies are still in their infancy, the perception is growing that the peoples of the Korean peninsula possess a culture uniquely their own, and one which is truly distinct from that of their better-known neighbours.

The choice of shamanism as the subject of the first volume was a natural one. As Prof. I. H. Kim points out in his lead-off article, the academic study of Korean shamanism has long suffered from neglect, distortion and cultural bias. The historical elite of the Korean peninsula have generally tended to scorn or ignore shamanism, particularly after the more sophisticated belief systems of Buddhism and Confucianism made their appearance. Hence, in historical literature there remain only glimpses of what must have been very widespread shamanistic practices in early Korean civilization. The first Western scholars of the subject, most of them missionaries, were universally cognizant of the force of shamanism among the Korean masses, but for obvious reasons, portrayed its beliefs as primitive and superstitious, and moreover, as a barrier to modernization. As Korea modernizes today, this attitude has not entirely disappeared, but as the late Dr. P. C. Hahm shows in his lengthy contribution to this volume, the shamanistic tradition is closely woven into the fabric of Korean life and is even now a determinant of the Korean world-view, as well as its family and social customs at all societal levels.

Most scholars, as represented in this collection by Prof. C. K. Chang, take the position that shamanism was an important part of Korea's Bronze Age culture, was intimately connected with early kingship, and should indeed be regarded as the indigenous religion of the Korean peoples. Throughout history, it has interacted with the imported traditions of Confucianism and Buddhism, and as Prof. C. S. Yu demonstrates in his essay on Korean Taoism, shamanism has affected and informed the development of these other creeds. Any understanding of the so-called New Religions of Korea would be difficult without some knowledge of shamanistic influences upon them.

For all these reasons, shamanism seemed the logical choice for a first volume on Korean religion. The editors, however, are under no illusion that the articles presented here constitute a comprehensive view of Korean shamanism. To begin with, we were limited by the lack of research in any language on certain key questions. Is there, or has there been, for instance, any real consensus in Korean shamanism on the existence of a Supreme Deity or Deities? What forms of historical-interaction existed between shamanism and a state which chose Confucianism or Buddhism as the orthodox ideology? How was the position of women in Korean society affected by shamanistic beliefs and practices? And is Korean shamanism distinct from other forms of folk religion, or is there even enough consistency of doctrine and practice to say that such an entity as "Korean shamanism" exists? Beyond questions like these, there is an entire range of issues which have yet to be raised by scholars, so that the articles in this collection may raise more questions than they answer. They are at least representative of the present concerns of Korean scholarship in the area. A second volume hopes to address some of these questions.

A second criterion for the selection of articles was our desire to introduce Korean scholars to a wider audience. With one exception, none of these articles has been previously available in a Western language, and hence, their accessibility to Western scholars and students has been severely limited. The authors are all leading experts in their particular fields and in our view, have contributed greatly to the understanding of Korean shamanism past and present. We have also consciously excluded from the collection some aspects of shamanism which might seem central to any study of the subject. One example of this is the fact that we include no fully detailed description of *kut* or other rituals. Our reasoning was that English-language studies are readily available, and we might mention for instance, *Shamans, Housewives and Other Restless Spirits: Women in Korean Ritual Life,* Laurel Kendall (University of Hawaii Press, 1985), and *Kut: Korean Shamanist Rituals,* Halla Pai Huhm. (Hollym International Corporation, New Jersey, 1980). In general, then, the subjects treated by our authors are those which have received little attention outside Korean academic circles.

We might note, finally, that because the collection is directed principally to students of world religion and comparative religion, we have avoided the use of Korean, and have provided notes only for the two articles (Yu, Yi) which have not been published elsewhere. In our *Acknowledgments,* we identify the original Korean sources and the specialist may wish to refer to them for the notes and bibliography.

However frustrating it has been to edit at long-distance a collection of this sort, the task has been rewarding. We have learned of the importance of shamanism in Korean history and culture; we have learned what areas of the field require more attention; and from the perspective of comparative religion, we have learned that the Korean experience is important.

Chai-shin Yu and Richard Guisso
Toronto, 1987

Korean Shamanism—
A Bibliographical Introduction

A mong scholars of Korean religion, there has long been a tendency to claim that in the earliest times the Korean people developed a unique religious tradition. The most prominent of these scholars are, Chae-ho Sin, who maintained that the indigenous religion was one of, and for, the educated classes, and Tong Ch'oe, who supported this view, suggesting that the indigenous religion could be traced to Sodo, where the lifestyle was highly religious and militaristic in character. Other scholars were less certain that this was the case and Nam-sŏn Choe, for instance, suggested that the original religion was one of Bulu, while Nŭng-hwa Yi saw it as "a religion of God or gods." Yi's important article, "A Study of Chosŏn Shamanism", suggested that the most ancient religious forms were, in fact, the precursors of Korean shamanism, and that a study of shamanism is therefore vital to the understanding of ancient Korean society. In-bo Chŏng supports this view.

In any case, the history of Korea's indigenous religion goes back a long way. The earliest literary evidence we have suggests that certain shamanistic rituals have changed little since their first performance. A long poem called "On the Old Shaman", appears in Yi Kyu-bo's *Tongguk Yi Sangguk chip,* and tells the story of an aged female shaman who was expelled from her home in the village of Kaegyŏng. Although Yi's poem shows the typical Confucian contempt for shamanism, it also contains rich detail about early shamanistic rituals and shows a close similarity even with today's ritual.

Another interesting source is the *Koryŏ-sa* which tells us that in the twelfth year of the reign of King Hyŏnjong (1021 A.D.), a nationwide ceremonial to bring rain was held with the participation of many shamans, and this constitutes the first record in an official source of such a practice. Similarly, the first Koryŏ king, Taejo, said in his "Ten Rules" that he wished to have two rituals performed: the *Yŏndong* which was a dedication to the Buddha, and the *P'algwan*, which was a shamanistic rite in honour of the Celestial King and five famous mountains and rivers. Both these ceremonials were to remain unchanged in the future according to the king's decree, and both resembled today's shaman practice which invokes worldly blessing and protection rather than other-worldly salvation. In fact, the *P'algwan* of the Koryŏ period closely parallels the modern *K'ŭn'kut* (Great Exorcism) and as we know from the *Koryŏ Dokyŏng,* the ritual was celebrated, as it is today, on the fifteenth of the lunar month. It also seems clear that this particular ritual dates from pre-Koryŏ times and was used in the Three Kingdoms period.

Another evidence of the longevity of this religious tradition is the fundamental similarlity not only of ritual form, but also of terminology. We find, for instance, that even prior to the Koryŏ period, such terms as *Sŏngwan* (supernatural being), *Langjung* (Male shaman), and *Hwarang* (an elite youth corps) had attained their present meanings, and of course, in early Silla, the ruler was called the *Ch'ach'a ung* which bore the meanings both of shaman and family elder.

A problem closely related to the ancient origin of shamanism is the suggestion by several scholars of the intimate connection between shamanism and the myth of Tan'gun as the progenitor of the Korean people. The principal adherents of this view, some of whom emphasize that this connection gives Korean shamanism a unique and even indigenous character, are such historians of ancient Korea as Nŭng-hwa Yi, Nam-sŏn Ch'oe, Ch'ae-ho Shin and Tong Ch'oe.

It should, however, be pointed out that a number of modern scholars disagree with this view. One example is Sok-chae Im who raised the following question:

> . . .Nŭng-hwa Yi based his theory that the origin of Korean shamanism lay in the Tan'gun myth on his investigation of the so-called "City of God" where Tan'gun established himself, and on his discovery of the annual performance by the earliest Korean tribes of the rituals of *Tongmaeng, Muchŏn, Yonggo*

and *Ch'an'gun,* which all have their origins in the Tan'gun mythology. He concluded that these four rituals constituted a "national" form of worship, and were closely related to the earliest concept of *Ch'ach'a ung* or shamanistic kingship.

However, as has been well established, the so-called "City of God" is a mythological concept, as is indeed, the existence of Tan'gun. The connection between them and the four rituals would be a tenuous one even if we granted their reality, and furthermore, we cannot be sure that the national rituals were really shamanistic in character. In fact, they probably resemble most closely early rituals of worship found in societies which have no shamanistic tradition whatsoever.

Prof. Im goes on to point out that such facts as the frequent use of an altar in non-shamanistic worship in early Korea, and the consistent pantheism, not monotheism, of shamanism does not prove the connection between Tan'gun and shamanism. The entire question remains one of scholarly debate, but it may be noted that Im's views are subject to criticism on the grounds that just because modern shamanism is principally concerned with exorcism, it may not be fair to exclude from the category of shamanism, the ancient rituals which were a form of celebration or worship of "heaven" or the "god(s)". Perhaps it is necessary, most of all, to reach a consensus on the definition of "shamanism", and even to examine the question of whether or not there existed in early times, a folk-religion in Korea which was distinct from "shamanism", but which eventually became amalgamated with it.

A useful approach to the study of Korean religion in general, and to the problems raised above in particular, is to examine early Korean writings, and a brief review may be helpful.

It is generally conceded that by about the first century B.C., the peoples of the Korean peninsula had developed a certain cultural consciousness and a sense of identity, and sometime later, began to write about their own history. The earliest recorded compilation of a state history occurred in 375 A.D. under King Kŭnchogo of Paekche, and in 545 A.D., King Yŏngyang of neighbouring Silla had a similar record

compiled. Koguryŏ was the latest of the Three Kingdoms to compile a
state history, but we are told that they produced about a hundred
volumes of history called *Yugi* in the years immediately following their
foundation. All three of these kingdoms undoubtedly based their official
state history on earlier records, and although these works are no longer
extant, the *Samguk sagi,* Korea's earliest remaining historical work, lists
several titles such as *Haedong kogi, Samhan kogi, Hwarang segi, Kogi,
Tan'gun ki,* etc. which were clearly works of history. Some may even
have dated from the earliest years of the Three Kingdoms period, and
the titles of some, like *Hwarang segi, Sŏn sa, Tan'gun ki and Sin'gi pisa*
indicate subject matter that was primarily religious and probably
shamanistic. It may not be too much to suggest that these early
bibliographical references demonstrate an early recognition of the
centrality of shamanism to cultural identity.

If it is true, and I believe this is the case, that the formal study of
shamanism can be dated to the early Three Kingdoms Period, it was not
until the early twentieth century that Korean scholars turned their
attention to the history of the study of native folklore and indigenous
religion. An important recent article by Kwŏn-hwan is entitled "A Study
of the Scholastic Concerns of the Silhak School of Modern Realism in
Korea", traces the work of post-Silhak scholars like Nŏng-hwa Yi and
Nam-sŏn Ch'oe in the 1920's, outlines the significance of their work on
shamanism, and even attempts to date the origins of Korean shamanism by comparision with German folklore. He saw the Korean tendency
to take pride in folk culture in the twentieth century as similar to that of
the Germans, and contrasted this with the British attitude, which either
neglected it or regarded it as inferior. He also proposed a *schema* to
define the importance of folk-culture, suggesting that its study could
provide:

1) knowledge by a culture of itself;
2) knowledge of the cultural achievements of the non-
governing segment of a society;
3) practical knowledge useful in dealing with the contemporary
world.

He goes on to examine the characteristics of the folkloric studies of Silhak scholars from the 1890s, and offers the following critical evaluations:

1) Much of their work was unsystematic and speculative, even unprofessional, since it largely ignored the written record and was also influenced at least in its choice of topics, by government authority.

2) The majority of Silhak scholars had little real appreciation of the importance of folkloric studies.

3) Folkloric studies comprised only a small part of the academic interests of the Silhak movement.

4) The scholars of the 1920's like Lee and Choe, accepted uncritically the definitions and methodology of the earlier Silhak scholars, thus perpetuating their mistakes.

Under these circumstances, it seems reasonable to widen our view of the history of Korean folkloric studies, and include among the practitioners such earlier scholars as Kyu-bo Yi (1168-1241), Iryŏn (1206-1289) and Sŭng-hyu Yi (1224-1302), thus demonstrating a much earlier recognition of the importance of mass culture in the formation of the national identity. The works of the above scholars, *Tongguk Yisangguk chip, Samguk yusa,* and *Chewang un'gi* offer ample evidence of this.

It is also interesting to note that various, if rather fragmentary, references in these works support our view that the interest of the literate classes in shamanism can be traced to the early Three Kingdoms period. There is also evidence later in the same period, of interaction and accommodation among shamanism, and such foreign influences as Chinese geomancy (*feng-shui*), Confucianism, Taoism and Buddhism. This is found not only in the sources cited above, but in the genre of casual writings like the *Tosŏn pigi,* and the works of Buddhist monks like Wŏnhyo and scholars like Ch'i-wŏn Ch'oe. In all these works there is recognition of the essential humanitarianism of such tenets of shamanism as protection from evil, the bringing about of worldly blessings, and the fostering of societal harmony.

Thus we might say that the study of shamanism extends back to remote times in Korean history but the study became genuinely systematic only in the twentieth century.

In looking at the developments of the twentieth-century,we might propose the following stages in the study of shamanism:

1) Formative Period of Systematic Study - 1900-1945;
2) Period of Preparation - 1946 - early 1960s;
3) Period of Rapid Scholastic Development - 1960 - 1970;
4) Period of Scholastic Transition - 1970 - 1980;
5) Period of Maturity - 1980 onward.

The formative period may be further subdivided into a discussion of studies by Westerners, by Japanese, and by Koreans, and it seems appropriate to deal with them in that order.

The principal Western interpreters of Korean shamanism had in common the advantage of direct observation and experience, as well as their Christian and/or missionary perspective. Studies of this sort began to appear around 1900 and perhaps the best example is H. B. Hulbert's series of six articles entitled "The Korean Mudang and Paksu" which appeared in *The Korea Review* (Vol. 3, numbers 4-9) beginning in 1903. H. G. Underwood, in his book, *The Call of Korea,* also dealt quite extensively with shamanism in a chapter entitled, "The People: Their Religious Life" in 1908. Both of these authors placed shamanism in the context of Korean folklore, and seemed in neither case to regard it as worthy of separate study. In 1932, C. A. Clark published *Shamanism: Religion of Old Korea,* and this work, while it relies to a great extent on Hulbert's observations, was the first by a Westerner to see shamanism as a key element in understanding Korea and to look at the religion from the perspective of its Korean form. Although this represented a step forward, it resembled several less detailed studies published around the same period, in regarding shamanism as primitive and superstitious. Virtually all studies by Westerners had as their underlying motivation a desire to understand shamanism's role in Korean society and the Korean consciousness as an aid to Christian evangelism.

Japanese studies in the formative period were also tendentious, though in their case the aim was to bolster their colonial regime. Several studies were produced or sponsored by such official bodies as the Imperial Academy, the Historical Society of Chosen, and the Office of the Government-general. Among the best-known of these works are the collections of Murayama Tomojun, published from 1929 under the titles *Chōsen no kijin* and *Chōsen no uranai to yogen*. Murayama's method was to use police stations throughout the country to collect his materials so there is a definite bias in his work, and it is thus not surprising that *Kijin [The Korean Ghost]* uses shamanism to demonstrate a lack of enlightenment and modernity on the part of the Korean people and to justify Japanese colonial rule.

While individual Japanese scholars like Akiba Takashi and Mishima Akihide also produced studies of shamanism, their fieldwork was by no means so extensive as that of Murayama who remained the leading Japanese figure in the field. His most important later work, the two-volume *Study of Korean Shamanism*, published in 1937 and 1938, used a more objective social-anthropology approach, and some of his work, for instance the publication of shaman chants both in Korean and Japanese languages, is academically important, even for scholars today.

We might point out, finally, that while some Japanese studies published in the period contain valuable on-the-spot observations, they suffer almost universally from a strong tendency to reflect the viewpoint of the colonial government and also from the lack of linguistic competence and knowledge of Korea's cultural originality on the part of the authors. The works of Mishima Akihide, *Mythological Foundation* (1939), *A Study of the Foundation Myths of Korea and Japan* (1943) and *A Study of the Hwarang in the Silla Kingdom* (1943) illustrate these problems while still demonstrating the usefulness of an anthropological approach.

Beginning after the so-called March First Movement in 1919, native Korean scholars became far more conscious of their cultural heritage, and as part of their contribution to a growing movement for Korean independence, turned their attention to Korean history and folklore. At the same time, several scholars began to familiarize themselves with Western methods of scientific enquiry and this is reflected in their studies of shamanism. Representative scholars of this period are Nam-sŏn Ch'oe, Nŭng-hwa Yi and Ch'ae-ho Sin who worked to find the spiritual origins of Korean culture by compiling bibliographic studies of early Korean civilization. Choe, in particular, was interested in identifying the Korean *Volkgeist* which appeared in ancient shamanism and the Tan'gun mythology, and in clarifying the unique character of Korean shamanism by comparing it to the primitive religions of neighbouring areas. We see this approach, for instance, in his studies of the *Samguk yusa*.

Nŭng-hwa Yi took a slightly different approach in his major works, *A Study of Korea's Divine Religion* (1922) and *A Study of Korean Shamanism* (Kaemyong, vol. 19, 1929). In them, he compiled the many extant literary references to shamanism in historical sources to show its centrality to Korean religious beliefs. His knowledge of Korean history made his studies particularly valuable.

Similar to Yi in method was Ch'ae-ho Sin whose major work *The Ancient History of Chosŏn* (1931) and the 1931 thesis "The Most Important Event of the Millenium in Korean History," and in his *Draft Study of Korean History* (1930), make clear the historical function of shamanism in Korean society, and with numerous bibliographical references, trace the fortunes of shamanism in Korean history.

Two other important scholars of this period, Ch'in-t'ae Son and Sŏk-ha Song, were also competent bibliographers, but supplemented their studies of shamanism with actual fieldwork which they explained using the methodology of social-anthropology and religio-folkloric studies. We see this clearly in such works as "The Culture of Ancient Chosŏn - What is Shamanism?" (1927), "The Primitive Beliefs of the Korean People" (1928), *A Compilation of the Sources for the Song of God in Chosŏn* (1930), and "A Study on the Sex of the Mountain God in Ancient Korea" (1934). Both Son and Song were conversant with the works and methods of Western scholars, and Song was especially active in excavation, field observation and the preservation of sources and artifacts of material culture.

His "Study on the God of the Wind" (1934) and "The Folklore of the Silla Kingdom" (1934) are particularly related to shamanism, and it is interesting to note that Son's *A Compilation of the Sources for the Song of God in Chosŏn* was the standard reference work on shaman chants until the 1965 publication of *Shaman Songs of the Kwanbuk*

Area by Sŏk-chae Im and Chu-gŭn Chang.

All these studies by Korean scholars were motivated by a sense of nationalism and the desire to define the roots of Korean culture. To some extent, they suffer from this bias and from the authors' conviction that shamanism was only a branch of folkloric studies, but they represent a step forward beyond the prejudice both of Japanese and Western missionary scholars.

We have called the period from 1945 to the 1960's a period of preparation in shamanistic study. During this period, the older generation of scholars were lost to the field by death (Song in 1948) or in other ways (Son was taken to North Korea during the Korean War). Although younger scholars like Sŏk-chae Im, Song-su Ch'o, Tong-gwŏn Im, and Chu-gŭn Chang took their place, their interest was folklore in general and the study of shamanism became stagnant. Little of interest was published with the exception of Nam-sŏn Ch'oe's *Questions and Answers on the Common Sense of Chosŏn* (1946) and Chae-wŏn Kim's *New Study on the Tan'gun Mythology* (1947), but during the 1950's, scholars began to improve their methodologies and there were signs that a new recognition of the importance of shamanism was beginning to appear.

The third period was characterized by rapid scholarly development. Numerous scholars turned their attention to shamanism and largely through fertile fieldwork on Cheju Island where the purest form of shamanistic practice continued to exist, they published some important studies. Most notable among them were Song-gi Chin's *Shaman Chants in the South* (1960) and *Mythology in the South* (1964). Yong-jun Hyŏn published "Legends of Cheju Island Shrines" (1962), "A Study of Shamanism on Cheju Island" (1963), "The Formation of Ponp'uri in Shamanistic Myth" (1963), "The Rule of Fortune in Shamanism" (1960), and "A Series on the Gods and their Characters in Cheju Shamanism" (1960). Chu-gŭn Chang also published his valuable "Study on the Characteristics of Cheju Island Shamanism" in 1964. The most notable studies of shamanism outside Cheju Island were T'ak-kyu Kim's *Study on Yonggo and Ogu* (1963) and T'ae-gon Kim's "Study on the Function of Ritual Prayer" (1964).

Almost all of these studies are somewhat elementary in interpretation, but the observations and description of shamanistic ritual is immensely valuable.

The last years of the 1960s saw a transition taking place as the number of scholars grew and began to apply to their studies the approaches not only of history and literature, but also of psychology, sociology, psychoanalysis and religious studies. Representatives of this emerging trend are Yŏl-gyu Kim's "A Study of Symbols in the Birth of Folk Religion" (1966) and "Shamanistic Village Rituals and the Mind of the Shaman" (1969). During the same period Pae-kang Whang used the Jungian theory of the archetype in his paper "The Archetype in Korea's Ancient Epic Literature" (1966), and "Research into Tan'gun Mythology" (1968). Pu-yŏng Yi produced two important papers called "The Phenomenon and Treatment of the Spirit of Death through Bibliographical References in Korean Shamanistic Sources" (1968), and "The Psycho-analytical Implications of the Procedures in Becoming a Shaman".

In the early 1970s, these transitional trends began to bear fruit as the number of young scholars continued to increase, learned societies were formed, and research continued to grow both in quantity and in quality. The works of this period applied social science and folkloric methods on a more sophisticated level than previously, and the finished product is characterized by a high standard of analysis and interpretation. Much of the work was built on the reference sources which appeared at this time, most notably on *A Comprehensive Report and Survey of Korean Folklore* (1969) which was the result of ten-year joint project by the Ministry of Information and Culture, and the Cultural and Anthropological Society of Korea. Similarly, Tae-gon Kim published a three-volume *Collection of Korean Shaman Chants* in 1971, 1976 and 1978, and Chung-yo Choe and Tae-sŏk Suh published *The Shaman Chants of Eastern Korea* in 1974.

With these resources at their disposal, scholars began to produce major studies. Among them are such works as the "Introduction to Korean Shamanism I-II" (1970-1971) by Sŏk-chae Im, *A Study of Korean Shamanism* (1978) by Kil-sŏng Ch'oe, and the two-volume

Folklore in the South—Shamanism on Cheju Island (1975) by Sŏng-gi Chin.

At the same time works which began to stress a theological viewpoint appeared. Among these are *The History and Structure of Korean Shamanism* (1975) by Tong-sik Yu, *A Study of Belief in Ancient Korea* (1970) by Pyŏng-gil Chang, and *The Study of Korean Folklore* (1973) by Kae-hong Pak.

A wide range of studies which used other disciplines to provide different perspectives on shamanism appeared throughout the 1970's. Those of greatest importance are Yŏl-gyu Kim's *The Study of Korean Mythology and Shamanism* (1977), *The Study of Ancient Korean Legend* (1973) by Sin-in Pak, "A Study of the Tan'gun Myth from a Folklore Perspective" (1971) by Tong-gwŏn Im, *The Mythology of the Korean People* (1972) by O-rŏng Yi, and *A Study of Korean Epic Literature* (1972) by P'ae-gang Hwang.

At the same time, the emergence of studies dealing with specific aspects of shamanism demonstrated the growing maturity of the field. In this connection, we might mention: "Shaman Songs of the Shinai Mountains" (1971) by Po-hyŏng Yi, and *The Korean Sense of Values—Shamanism and Educational Philosophy* (1977) by In-whoe Kim. Other examples are "Social Function and the Theatrical Character of the Kut" (1977) by Sang-il Yi and *The Theatrical Character of Kut in the Seoul Area* (1975) by Ru-si Hwang.

Finally, there were several studies which looked at shamanism from a psychological or medico-anthropological point of view. Most notable are: "The Analytical Study of Shamanistic Treatment of the Spirit of Death" (1970) by Pu-yŏng Yi, "Kut and Psychotherapy" (1972) by Kwang-il Kim, and *Modern Medical Treatment and Medical Culture in a Remote Korean Village* (1978) by Sun-yŏng Yun.

The final stage of shamanistic studies, that of genuine maturity, began only about 1980, and is dated from the appearance of three works of great significance. These were: *A Study of Korean Shaman Chants* (1980) by Tae-sŏk Sŏh, *A Dictionary of Cheju Island Shamanism* (1980) by Yong-jun Hyŏn, and *The Study of Korean Shamanism* (1981) by T'ae-gon Kim. All are of high quality and great value, and each makes a special contribution to the field. Thus, for instance, the chapter on "The Chae-sŏk-bon-p'uri" in Sŏh's work compares the transmission of shaman chants in various areas and shows the effect of cultural and historical factors in the variant forms of their transmission. He also makes clear the place of mythology in shamanistic literature.

The comparative character of this work is important, as is the connection shown between current ritual and the mythology of Tan'gun ahd Chumung. In a more general sense, his work tells us much about the transmission of oral tradition and its place in the folk-consciousness of the Korean people. Hyŏn's *Dictionary* divides the ritual activities of Cheju Island shamanism into the three broad categories of: *K'ŭn-kut* or major exorcism, *chagŭn-kut* or lesser exorcism, and *tang-kut* or chamber-exorcism. He shows the distinctions among the three types and reproduces the chants in each. Another interesting aspect of his work is his introduction of the Cheju dialect and his copious annotations and full appendix provide hitherto unavailable information on the idiom, costuming and accoutrements of Cheju shamans. For the first time, the terminology of the Cheju shamans is made fully comprehensible.

Kim's *Study of Korean Shamanism* breaks new ground in a similar way, particularly by his systematic rearrangement of the structures of thought, prototypes and bibliography of Korean shamanism. He provides in his work a chronology of the development of shamanistic studies and an index of shamanistic terminology. In his work, we also see the value of various methodologies which can be applied with profit to the study of shamanism.

In sum, studies of shamanism by Korean scholars have now reached a level of maturity which demonstrates the value of these studies in shedding light upon the Korean experience, both past and present.

Bibliography

Akamatsu Jizo and Akiba Takashi. *Chōsen huzoku no kenkyū* (A Study
  of Korean Shamanism), 2 vols., Seoul: Ōsaka yagō shoten, 1937,
  1938.

Chang Chu-gŭn. "Chejudo musok ŭi chiyŏksŏng e taehayŏ (A Study of
  Regional Characteristics of Shamanism on Cheju Island)," *Chejudo*
  15, Cheju: Cheju Province Office, 1964.

Chang Pyŏng-gil. *Han'guk koyu sinang yŏn'gu* (A Study of Indigenous
  Beliefs of Korea), Seoul: Seoul National University, 1978.

Chin Sŏng-gi. *Namguk ŭi muga* (Shaman Chants of the South), Cheju:
  Cheju minsok munhwa yŏn'guso, 1960.

————. *Namguk ŭi sinhwa* (Myths of the South), Seoul: Arim
  ch'ulp'ansa, 1965.

————. *Namguk ŭi minsok: Chejudo Minsok* (Folklore of the South:
  Shamanism on Cheju Island), Seoul: Kyohaksa, 1975.

Cho Chi-hun. "Nusŏktan sinsu tangchip sinang yŏn'gu (A Study of the
  Beliefs of the Stone-piled Platform, the Divine Tree, and the
  Shrine), *Mullidae nonmunjip,* Seoul: Korea University, 1963.

Ch'oe Chŏngyŏ and Sŏ Tae-sŏk. *Tonghaean muga* (Shaman Chants of
  the East-coast Region), Taegu: Hyŏngsol ch'ul-p'ansa, 1974.

Ch'oe Kil-sŏng. *Han'guk musok ŭi yŏn'gu* (A Study of Korean
  Shamanism), Seoul: Asea munhwasa, 1978.

Ch'oe Nam-sŏn. "Samguk yusa haeje (A Bibliographical Introduction
  to the *Samguk yusa*)," *Chŭngbo Samguk yusa,* Seoul: Minjung
  sŏgwan, 1946.

————. *Chosŏn sangsik mundap* (Questions and Answers on the
  Common Sense of Chosŏn), Seoul: Tongmyongsa, 1947.

Ch'oe Tong. *Chosŏn sanggo minjoksa* (A History of Ancient Korean People), Seoul: Tongguk munhwasa, 1966.

Chŏng In-bo. *Chosŏnsa yŏn'gu* (A Study of Chosŏn History), Seoul: Seoul sinmunsa, 1946.

Clark, C. A. *Shamanism: Religion of Old Korea*, 1929; reprint, Seoul: Christian Literature Society of Korea, 1961.

Han'guk minsok chonghap pogosŏ (A General Report of Korean Folklore), 12 vols., Seoul: Ministry of Culture and Information, 1969-1980.

Hsü Ching. *Kao-ri t'u-ching*, 1124; reprint, Seoul: Ewha Women's University, 1970.

Hulbert, H. B. "The Korean Mudang and Pansu," *The Korean Review*, vol. 3, no. 4-9, Seoul: Methodist Publishing House, 1903.

Hwang Lu-si. *Kut ŭi yŏn'gŭksŏng* (The Theatrical Nature of *Kut*), master's thesis at Ewha Women's University, Seoul, 1978.

Hwang P'ae-gang. "Han'guk kodae sŏsa munhak ŭi archetype (The Archetypes in Ancient Korean Narrative Literature)," *Munho* 4, Seoul: Kŏn'guk University, 1966.

_____. "Tan'gun sinhwa ui han yŏn'gu (A Study of Tan'gun Myth)," *Paeksan hakpo* 3, Seoul: Paeksan hakhoe, 1967.

_____. *Han'guk sŏsa munhak yŏn'gu* (A Study of Korean Narrative Literature), Seoul: Tan'guk University, 1972.

Hyŏn Yong-jun. "Chejudo tang sinhwa ko (A Study of Myths of Cheju Island Shrines)," *Chejudo* 3, 1962.

_____. "Musok sinhwa ponp'uri ŭi hyŏngsŏng (The Formation of *Ponp'uri* in Shamanistic Myths)," *Kugŏ kungmunhak* 26, Seoul: Kugŏ kungmunhak hoe, 1963.

_____. "Chejudo musok ko (A Study of Shamanism on Cheju Island)," *Chejudo* 10, 1963.

————. "Chejudo ŭi mujŏm pop (The Rule of Shaman Fortune-telling on Cheju Island)," *Chejudo* 12, 1963.

————. "Chejudo musin ŭi sŏngkkyŏk kwa sint'ong (The Genealogy and Characteristics of the Shamanistic Gods of Cheju Island)," *Chejudo* 17, 1964.

————. *Chejudo musok charyo sajŏn* (A Dictionary of Materials on Shamanism on Cheju Island), Seoul: Sin'gu munhwasa, 1980.

Im Sŏk-chae and Chang Chu-gŭn. *Kwanbuk chibang muga* (Shaman Songs of the Kwanbuk Region), *Muhyŏng munhwajae charyo* (Materials on Intangible Cultural Assets), no. 13, Seoul: Ministry of Education, 1966.

Im Sŏk-chae. "Han'guk musok yŏn'gu sŏsŏl (Introductory Remarks on the Study of Korean Shamanism)," *Asea yŏsŏng yŏn'gu* 9, 10, Seoul: Sungmyŏng Women's University, 1970, 1971.

Im Tong-gwŏn. "Tan'gun sinhwa ŭi minsokhak chŏk koch'al (Tan'gun Myth Seen from the Perspective of Folklore)," *Hyeam Yu Hong-nyŏl paksa hwagap nonch'ong,* Seoul, 1971.

In Kwŏn-hwan. *Han'guk minsokhaksa* (A History of the Study of Folklore in Korea), Seoul: Yŏlhwadang, 1978.

Iryŏn. *Samguk yusa* (History of the Three Kingdoms), 1281-3; reprint, Seoul: Tongguk munhwasa, 1969.

Kim Chae-won (or Kim Chewon). *Tan'gun sinhwa ŭi sin yŏn'gu* (A New Study of the Tan'gun Myth), Seoul: Chŏngŭmsa, 1947.

Kim In-hoe. *Han'gugin ŭi kach'igwan: musok kwa kyoyuk ch'ŏrhak* (The Sense of Value of the Korean People—Shamanism and Philosophy of Education), Seoul: Munumsa, 1979.

Kim Kwang-il. "Kut kwa chŏngsin chi'ryo (*Kut* and Psychotherapy)," *Munhwa illyuhak* 5, Seoul, 1972.

Kim Pu-sik. *Samguk sagi* (The History of the Three Kingdoms), 1145; reprint.

Kim T'ae-gon. "Ch'ugwŏnmun ŭi kinŭng ko (On the Function of Prayers of Supplication)," *Kobong* 12, Seoul: Kyŏŏnghi University, 1964.

Kim T'ae-gon. *Han'guk muga chip* (A Collection of Shaman Chants of Korea), vols. 1-1, Iri: Wŏn'gwang University, 1971, 1976; vols. 3-4, Seoul: Chimmundang, 1979.

_____. *Han'guk musok yŏn'gu* (A Study of Korean Shamanism), Seoul: Chimmundang, 1981.

Kim T'aek-kyu. "Yŏnggo wa ogu e taehayŏ (A Study of *Yŏnggo* and *Ogu*," *Kŭgo kungmunhak* 20, 1963.

Kim Yŏl-gyu. "Minsok sinang ŭi saengsaeng sangjing yŏn'gu (A Study of birth Symbols in Folk Religion)," *Asea yŏn'gu* 22, Seoul: Korea University, 1966.

_____. "Minsok purakche wa kŭ min'gan sago (Shamanistic Festivals of Village and Popular Minds)," *Inmun kwahak* 12, Seoul: Yonsei University, 1969.

_____. *Han'guk sinhwa wa musok yŏn'gu* (A Study of Korean Mythology and Shamanism), Seoul: Ilchogak, 1977.

Koryŏsa (The History of Koryo), 1452; reprint, Seoul: Yonsei University, 1955.

Mishima Akihide. *Kenkoku shinwa ronko* (A Study of Foundation Myth), Tokyo: Meguro shoten, 1937.

_____. *Nissen shinwa densetsu no kenkyū* (A Study of the Myth and Legend of Korea and Japan), Osaka: Yanagihara shoten, 1943.

_____. *Shiragi karō no kenkyū* (A Study of the Hwarang of Silla), Tokyo: Sanseido, 1943.

Murayama Tomojun. *Chōsen no kijin* (The Ghost of Korea), Seoul: Chōsen sōtokufu, 1929.

_____. *Chōsen no bokusen to yogen* (The Divination and Prophecy of Korea), Seoul: Chōsen sōtokufu, 1933.

Pak Kye-hong. *Han'guk minsok yŏn'gu* (A Study of Korean Folklore), Taegu: Hyŏngsol ch'ulp'ansa, 1973.

Pak Si-in. *Han'guk sanggo sŏlhwa ŭi yŏn'gu—t'aeyang sinhwa ŭi idong ŭl chungsim ŭro* (A Study of Ancient Korean Legend with the Emphasis on the Sun Myth), Ph.D. dissertation at Seoul National University, 1973.

Sin Ch'ae-ho. "Chosŏn yŏksa sang ilch'ŏnnyŏn rae che iltae sagŏn (The Most Important Event in the Second Millenium A.D. in Korean History)," *Chosŏnsa yŏn'gu ch'o* (A Draft of Studies on Korean History), Seoul: Yŏnhaksa, 1930.

————. *Chosŏn sanggosa,* Seoul: Chongno sŏgwan, 1948.

Sŏ Tae-sŏk. *Han'guk muga ŭi yŏn'gu* (A Study of Korean Shaman Chants), Seoul: Munhak kwa sasang sa, 1980.

Son Chin-t'ae. "Chosŏ china minjok ŭi wŏnsi sinang yŏn'gu (A Study of the Primitive Beliefs of the Peoples of Korea and of China)," *Yŏsi* 1, 1928.

————. *Chōsen shinka ihen* (A Compilation of Extant Songs of God of Korea), Tokyo: Kyōdo kenkyū sha, 1930.

————. "Chosŏn kodae sansin ŭi sōng e taehayō (A Study of the Sex of the Mountain Gods of Ancient Korea)," *Chindan hakpo* 1, 1934.

Song Sŏk-ha. "P'ungsin ko (A Study of the Wind God), *Chidan hakpo* 1, 1934.

————. "Silla ŭi minsok (The Folklore of Silla)," *Chogwang* 1, 1935.

Underwood, H. G. *The Call of Korea,* New York: Fleming H. Revell, 1908.

Yi Kyu-bo. *Tongguk Yi sangguk chip* (A Compilation of Works of Minister Yi of the Eastern Country), 1251; reprint, Seoul: Tongguk munhwasa, 1958.

Yi Nung-hwa. "Chosŏn sin'gyo wŏllyu ko (On the Origin of the Religion of God of Korea," *Sarim* 7-3, 1922.

_____. "Chosŏn musok ko (A Study of Korean Shamanism," *Kyemyŏng* 19, Seoul: Kyemyŏng Club, 1927.

Yi Ŏ-ryŏng. *Han'gugin ŭi sinhwa* (The Myth of the Korean People), Seoul: Sŏmundang, 1972.

Yi Po-hyŏng. "Sinawi kwŏn ŭi muak (Shaman Music of the Sphere of *Sinawi*)," *Munhwa illyuhak* 4, Seoul, 1971.

Yi Pu-yŏng. "Han'guk musok kwan'gye charyo esŏ pon saryŏng ŭi hyŏnsang kwa ch'iryo (The Phenomenon and the Treatment of the Spirit of Death Seen in Materials about Korean Shamanism)," *Sin'gyŏng chŏngsin ŭihak* 7-2, Seoul, 1968.

_____. "Immu kwajŏng ŭi myŏt kaji t'ŭkching e taehan punsŏk simnihak chŏk koch'al (An Analytic-psychological Study on Some Characteristics of the Procedure of Initiation of a Shaman)," *Munhwa illyuhak* 2, 1969.

_____. "Saryong ŭi musok chŏk ch'iryo e taehan punsŏk simnihak chŏk yŏn'gu (An Analytic-psychological Study of Shamanistic Treatment of the Spirit of Death)," *Ch'oesin ŭihak* 13-1, 1970.

Yi Sang'il. "Kut ŭi Yŏn'gŭksŏng kwa sahoejok kinŭng (The Theatrical Nature and the Social Function of *Kut*)," *Segye ŭi munhak* 2-1, 1977.

Yi Sŭng-hyu. *Che wang un'gi* (A Book of Poems on Emperors and Kings), 1274-1308; reprint, Seoul: Han'gukhak munhŏn yŏn'guso, 1973.

Yu Tong-sik. *Han'guk mugyo ŭi yŏksa wa kujo* (The History and Structure of Korean Shamanism), Seoul: Yonsei University.

Yun Sun-yong. *Hyŏndae ŭiryo wa han'guk nongch'on ŭi ŭiryo munhwa* (Modern Medical Treatment and A Medical Culture in Korean Rural Villages), Seoul: Ewha University, 1978.

An Introduction to Korean Shamanism

$$\overline{\overline{}}$$

S hamanism is perhaps the most ancient, and in both East and West, the most ubiquitous of religious phenomena. It has often co-existed with other forms of magic, superstition and religion, so that a simple and discrete definition of its meaning and character is not easy. To compound the problem, shamanism in Korea has usually been regarded as akin to superstition, while in Japan, it was given a more respectable position as a set of public religious activities which evolved into National Shinto.

In both settings, however, Eliade's notion of shamanism as "archaic techniques of ecstasy" seems to apply, since in most cases the shamans themselves occupy the position corresponding to "spirit" in other forms of magico-religious ecstasy and are therefore distinct from more "orthodox" religious practitioners. In the Korean case, there are regional variations so that, for instance, in the north only male shamans are regarded as being truly possessed by the spirit while in the south, the opposite is true. In Cheju Island, generally regarded as the home of the purest form of Korean shamanism, one finds unique observances and attitudes. These will be discussed below.

A final point to be made before passing on to a brief history of Korean shamanism is that in the more primitive areas of the Korean countryside, shamanism represents even today the most basic reality of religious experience. Here, shamans assume Banzaroff's threefold role of priest, medicine-man and prophet, and in addition, promote folk-art and folk-culture. In Cheju Island, shamanism is virtually the sole transmitter of Korean myth.

It is generally conceded that shamanism existed in the Korean peninsula well before the tenth century B.C., and archeological evidence in fact suggests that it was part of Bronze Age culture. Just as is the case today in remote areas of the countryside, shamanistic ceremonies to propitiate local gods of field and forest were held, and though in ancient times, both sexes served as shaman, today, females invariably fill this role.

In time, the scattered communities coalesced into the kingdoms of Koguryŏ, Paekche and Silla, and it is interesting to note, as Professor W.Y. Kim assumes, that the well-known golden crowns of the Silla era were used not only as symbols of kingship, but were worn also as the sign of the chief shaman of the kingdom. Literary evidence makes it very clear that sacerdotal functions were integral to Sillan kingship and we find in the *Samguk sagi* for instance, that the second king of Silla, Namhae Kŏsŏgan, was also called *Ch'ach'a ung* or High Shaman. Contemporary Chinese sources bear out this designation and the *San-kuo Chih* states: "In Silla, the king was called Kosagon, or termed *Ch'ach'a Ung* or *Ch'ach'ung*". Kim Tae-mun, an eighth-century Silla scholar commenting on the passage, suggested that, "in the national [Korean] language, "Ch'ach'a ung" means shaman."

Another title for the Sillan ruler was *maripkan* which means, literally, "seat-marker" and refers to the marks which indicated the proper seating positions of ruler and courters during court cere-monials. Since these ceremonials were religious in character, the term is yet another indication of the sacerdotal role of the Sillan ruler.

Other instances of the religious power of kings in the Three Kingdoms period are numerous, and are not restricted to Silla. One of the best-known of these, concerns the attack on Koguryŏ by the T'ang emperor T'ai-tsung in 646 A.D., the fourth year of King Pojang. In this incident, the Chinese, with their vast numerical superiority, were repulsed in their attack on the fortress of Yodong after a shaman prophesied to King Pojang that the fortress would be saved if the proper rituals were dedicated to Chumong, the reputed founder of the city. The Chinese defeat was attributed to Chumong's intervention and the shamanistic character of the ruler could no doubt be viewed as a source of unity and resolve among his people.

During the Koryŏ period (918-1392 A.D.), there arose the first recorded opposition to shamanism. This was due largely to the rising influence of Confucianism, particularly in court circles. Especially as the Chinese examination system, with its wholly Confucian curriculum, became the requisite for appointment to civil office, successful scholars began to criticize what they regarded as excessive shamanistic influence upon the women of the palace—both queens and princesses. One of the best-known Confucian scholars of his time, Yi Kyu-bo, recounts the organized shamanistic rituals of the period and tells of how one particular shaman claimed to be a shaman-god and claimed that his ritual dancing had reached the level of the "grand roof-beam" [of the cosmos].

In spite of the contempt for shamanism among the rationalistic Confucian scholars, it seems to have harmonized well with Buddhism which became something of a state religion during the Koryŏ period. However, with the founding of the Yi dynasty in 1392, the situation changed. The *Kyŏngguk taejŏn,* promulgated in the first lunar month of 1470, was to be the basis of all Korean law and state organization until the twentieth century. It was highly Confucian in bias, and helped to Confucianize society, particularly at the upper levels. Thus, for instance, the Buddhist monks and shamans who had been considered as an upper class during the Koryŏ period, were relegated to the lower class of merchants, artisans, butchers and entertainers. Eventually their freedom of mobility was restricted as they were forbidden access to the capital and prevented from carrying out ceremonies and rituals out-of-doors.

Another aspect of Confucianism which took root in this period was ancestor-worship with sacrifices extending usually to the fourth generation. Needless to say, the spread of this practice deepened the paternalism of society, affecting attitudes toward the aged and also toward women. As women were increasingly barred from participation in such areas as education, and social activities with men, one of the few remaining avenues for their self-realization was found in shamanism.

During the Yi dynasty, it seems that shamanism was less widely practised than before at all levels of society, but it was certainly not eradicated from people's minds. Instead, the quality of shamanistic observance declined: partly because of the influence of the uneducated women who were the chief practitioners, and partly because the religion itself was regarded as little more than superstition and occupied the status almost of an outlawed doctrine. The coming of Christianity in the nineteenth century dealt shamanism yet another blow since the missionaries refused to accord it any legitimate status whatsoever, and in the subsequent vogue for modernization, it came to be seen more than ever as old fashioned superstition and even as heresy.

The results of this attitude are seen in the following table which presents the data of a statistical survey of Korean religions undertaken in 1972.

Statistical Survey of Korean Religions, 1972

Name of religious group	Number of clergy	Number of followers
1. Buddhism	18,629	7,990,000
2. Protestant	17,562	3,460,000
3. Roman Catholic	3,478	790,000
4. Confucianism	11,831	4,420,000
5. Ch'ŏndogyo	1,526	720,000
6. Wŏn Buddhism	805	680,000
7. Taejonggyo	55	150,000
8. Miscellaneous (mostly new)	4,102	1,410,000
Total	57,997	19,610,000

A few remarks about the table seem to be in order. First of all, while Confucianism is included, it is debatable whether it should be considered a religion or a political and social ideology. The number of "clergy" given is no more than an estimate since those who preside in

Confucian ceremonials do not form permanent, recognizable group-
ings in the manner, for instance, of Buddhist monks. Secondly,
Ch'ŏndogyo, Wŏn Buddhism, and Taejonggyo are all of recent origin in
Korea, with Wŏn a splinter group of mainstream Buddhist sects, and
Ch'ŏndogyo (Religion of the Heavenly Way), a unique religion
indigenous to Korea. In any case, it is clear from comparative data that
while the adherents of Buddhism vastly outnumber those of Christianity, Protestantism is the fastest growing religious group.

The survey did not provide information on shamanism, pre-
sumably because of the difficulty of gathering data. However, according
to the Organization of Korean Shamans, there are about 50,000
registered shamans in the oganization with between 100-200,000
followers.

It might be useful now to complete this survey of Korean
Shamanism by looking at some aspects of shamanistic belief and
practice, with special reference to Cheju Island where one finds,
perhaps, the purest form of shamanism.

1. *Shrine Shamanism*—It should first be noted that in shamanism
the concept of "God" is multiple, rather akin to the folk religion of
ancient Greece. The variety of shamanistic "gods" is great and the
form of an individual deity may vary from region to region. As
previously observed, shrine ritual is a product of ancient tribal rites,
most often arising from annual tribal festivals. The form has changed
little down to the present day. One source, for instance, states that the
Tongmaen ritual practised in the Koguryŏ period (37 B.C. - 668 A.D.),
employed a female statue in a cave. Even today on Cheju Island there
are cave-shrines dedicated to female deities. In many cases, village
rituals continued to be observed at the time of the full moon, and as
Eliade points out in regard to other societies, the female deity, the
earth and the full moon represent the principle of fertility and birth.
We might add, however, that shamanistic activity of this sort was
severely curtailed under Confucian influence during the Yi dynasty
from the late fourteenth century onwards, and is today declining even
more rapidly due to industrialization and modernization.

2. *Household Shamanism*—As indicated earlier, the observance of

primitive shamanism, as a unification of religion and state, was not able to continue under the Confucian state, which was much more concerned with the practical realities of politics. Thus shamanism had to become a sort of "underground" religion, revered only by women and members of the lower classes. In spite of this, several sacred figures of folk-belief were found in countryside homes. These were:

a) Ch'ŏ-Yong (The Spirit of the Forefathers)

The location of the shrine, or Ch'ŏ-Yong, is in the innermost chamber of the house. This is uniformly in the same place everywhere in the country, even though the names and the formation of the shrines differ from one another. For example, in the southern part of the country in Kyŏngbuk Province, it is called *San Sin* (God of Birth), whereas in Honam Province it is called *Ogari Sin* (God of Pots). The most common "Household Shrine" shapes are the pot, the gourd and the sack. Usually they are filled with barley in summer and with rice in winter as an appeasement for the god(s).

b) Sŏng-Ju (The God of the Household)

Sŏng-ju includes within its meaning the three ideas of the god protecting the house from evil, the god fostering the fortune of the house, and the god safeguarding the head of the family. The placement of Sŏng-ju varies in different parts of the country, though in most areas, it is placed in a corner of the wooden floor, or hallway, which is located on the way to the rooms. It is also filled with barley or rice according to the season of the year and it is still customary in modern cities in October for women to make rice cakes and to share them together with their neighbors. While not actually, or consciously, a shaman ritual, it probably derives from such early rituals and has probably become simply customary.

c) Cho-wang (God of the Kitchen)

Cho-wang, or god of the kitchen, is regarded also as the god of the sacred fire. The shamanistic rituals surrounding him are held in the center of the kitchen where the kitchen deities are located. Particularly in Honam Province, in the southern area of the country, the first thing the women do after daybreak is to show reverence to the kitchen god with an offering of a bowl of pure water at the so-called "altar" in the kitchen. Cho-wang is also called the God of Woman.

d) T'ŏju and ŏp (God of the Backyard)

T'ŏju was the god of the residence lot. In most areas, uniformly, a pot filled with rice or barley was placed in the backyard. Op was the god of fortune. For example, a large snake was regarded as good fortune, as were also toads. If he saw a snake, the landholder usually made a prognostication, and if the snake left his property, his good fortune went along with it. This kind of traditional shamanistic thinking is, however, fading away under the influence of modernization.

II. A Survey of Shamanism on Cheju Island

A. Topography

Cheju Island is the largest island situated off the southern coast of the peninsula. Elliptical in shape, one hundred kilometers in circumference, the island has a population of approximately 400,000. The three conditions of its situation—its area, population, and distance from the mainland—have caused the island to preserve the old characteristics intact from outside influence.

Historically, Cheju Island came under the control of Paekche during the period of the Three Kingdoms, and later was governed autonomously under the control of the United Silla (669-918 A.D.). During the Koryŏ Dynasty, the Mongols occupied the island for 29 years in order to use it for raising horses and as a preparatory base for conquering Japan. In some periods, the island was also connected to Okinawa and Japan.

At present, there are 2 colleges, 20 high schools, 32 junior high schools and 102 primary schools on the island. It has been modernized as a tourist site, but as one enters farming and fishing villages, one finds that the old cultural types are still preserved.

B. *Mudangs* or Shamans

According to a survey conducted in 1959, there were a total of 227 *mudangs,* 99 males and 128 females, among a population of 280,000. Among them, there were 96 hereditary shamans, 80 spontaneous ones, and 51 of unknown origin. The average age of those shamans was calculated to be 51. The survey also indicated that some 100 female shamans practiced obstetrics and pediatrics. The shamans in general on the island do not leap with ecstasy, nor do they make oracles. They are usually dressed as priests, but there are a few instances in which they are dressed as gods. In the latter cases, they manifest some signs of theatricality. Shamans are called *shimbang* on Cheju Island.

C. Shrines

1. *Ponhyang-dang* or Village-Shrine

There is a *Ponhyang-dang* in every village in principle, and at present about two-thirds of such shrines, 150 in number, are preserved. This type of shrine is quite often a sacred tree, where village wives get together to conduct a community ritual, usually twice a year, in spring and fall, but in some villages it is held four times a year.

2. *Iret-tang* or Seventh-Day-Shrine

On the 7th and 27th days of each month, women perform a personal rite offering individual prayers. There are 95 such shrines on the island, and the goddess worshipped is supposed to be a daughter of the Dragon King, practicing the treatment of infantile disorders, eye infections, skin diseases, and digestive malfunctions. This practice seems to have been derived from the diseases indigenous to the island.

3. *Yŏdŭret-tang* or Eighth-Day-Shrine

This is the type of shamanism worshipping serpents and is widely spread all over the island. About 20 such shrines still exist in the southeastern part of the island. Individual shrines hold prayer rituals on the 8th, 18th, and 28th of each month.

4. *Haesin-dang* or Seagod-Shrine

These shrines are to be found along the beach, where fishermen and women-divers perform the rites. The godhood of such shrines is so far unidentified. They are generally called "Grandmother" or

"Grandfather" of the sea, and are prayed to for safety on the sea. According to the survey, some 40 shrines still exist on the island.

5. *P'oje-dan* or *P'oje*-Altar

In principle, each village is supposed to have such an altar, and at present about two-thirds of villages are in possession of such altars. This is the shrine where men perform a ritual service jointly for the community in January of each year, in compliance with Confucian ritual services. In some villages, there are well-kept altars, while others make their ritual offerings by placing food on a certain high spot in the village area. Their gods are considered to be protectors of their villages or to be the native gods of the village. No names have been given to such shrines and the legend of their origin has not been found. Two forms of ritual are performed, with men practising Confucian rituals and women, shamanistic rituals.

On the peninsula, Confucian village-rites still exist, with men as the officiating priests. However, since Cheju Island has female priests, it can be concluded that women's position is higher on Cheju Island than on the mainland.

D. *Ponp'uri* or the Myth of Shamanism

1. The Definition and Classification of *Ponp'uri*.

Ponp'uri is a shaman epic, explaining the origin and history of the gods. Three types of *ponp'uri* exist. One is the *ponp'uri* of the gods of shrines, which is the legend of village-gods of protection. These gods are summoned by *simbang,* a priest of the shrine, on a certain ritual date. Another type is a general which is commonly called *kut,* or a shaman-rite to be conducted by anyone and anywhere. This is performed to exorcise evil spirits by invoking the god of agriculture or the god of wealth and the god of disease. Anyone who performs as *simbang* should be able to recite a great many lines of *ponp'uri,* of which there are more than 250 pages. The third and last type of the *ponp'uri* is the ancestral legend, which is the myth of the protective god of the family, often recited at the time of family-ritual.

2. The Essence and Function of *Ponp'uri*

Ponp'uri is spontaneous in its origin. The myth, which is recited to music, is the history of a personified god and is a component of the ritual. The recitation of it is supposed to summon gods down to the earth and to please them. Since it explains the history and character of gods, it will lead to knowledge of the way gods are to be treated. Since to know the way of exorcising the god of disease is a form of medical theory, the holding of a ritual, reciting *ponp'uri*, welcoming benevolent gods, and expelling evil spirits becomes clinical treatment in itself. This is the religious function of *ponp'uri* and at the next stage, it also plays a literary function. By reciting it, both gods and human beings are pleased, which will increase the efficacy of the ritual. In this tradition alone, *ponp'uri* has helped to develop national art by giving birth to myths, to *p'an-sori*—a type of Korean classical opera—and to drama. The social aspect of *ponp'uri*'s function is hard to discover, since shamanism has lost its leading role in society, but there are some elements of Buddhism in *ponp'uri*, which is a definite sign that Buddhist monks exploited native *ponp'uri* in order to propagate their religion.

3. The Form of *Ponp'uri* Expression

The form of *ponp'uri* expression is basically the rhythm of 4 syllables in succession, and is adjusted for the sake of recitation with meaningless sounds *ah* and *eh* inserted to maintain the basic rhythm. For increased rhythmical effect, a *chang-go,* a type of Korean drum, accompanies the recitation. Repetition, antitheses, hyperbole, and hackneyed expressions abound in the lines recited, and there are many dialogue forms included in them also. And occasionally, shamans play the roles of gods while performing dramatic rituals.

4. The Formation and Motifs of *Ponp'uri*

Approximately 300 shrines on the island have been given the names of the gods. The names of gods, stories of how they settled in those shrines, the function of the god in helping human beings, the date of the god's festival, family names in the community, words of prayers—these gradually combine to form *ponp'uri*. Among these elements of *ponp'uri*, the legend of a god's settlement in a shrine is the most important element. About 60 legends of this type have been collected, but on closer observation, no more than 20 motifs can be derived from these 60 myths. The important ones are: a.) the emergence of male gods from earth, b.) the hunting and flesh-eating life of male gods, c.) settlement at the place of an arrow's fall, d.) the entry of a female god into the island after drifting on the sea, e.) the marriage of male god to female god, f.) the female god's encouragement of, and recommendation of agriculture to male gods, g.) the rice diet of the female god, h.) the conflict between male gods and female gods arising from a difference in tastes, i.) stories of a god's drifting on the sea and his acts of heroism, j.) the guidance of a female god's chosen people in religious life, etc. These motifs do not exist by themselves, but exist in different combinations, and are used as the *ponp'uri* of a particular shrine. On the mainland, the primary motif which is found is how the Son-of-Heaven came down to the top of a mountain, but on Cheju Island gods are believed to have emerged from the earth. Such a motif of emergence is also found in Oceania. Male gods lead hunting and carnivorous lives, whereas goddesses lead a rice-eating life in a capital city or in the state of the Dragon King, before finally coming to the island. This is often interpreted as suggesting that the original hunting culture of the island was later supplemented by the female occupation of agriculture. Simultaneously, this motif reflects the nature and the history of cultural life on the island.

5. The Myth of Three Ancestral Families

Koryŏsa (the history of the Koryŏ Dynasty) records the myth of three ancestral families, the Go, the Yang, and the Pu. According to the myth, three gods emerged from the earth, hunting and eating flesh, while three goddesses entered the island in a boat, bringing with them the seeds of five grains, calves and ponies. They wedded the three ancestral gods and became the progenitors of the island. The Three-Holes, about ten centimeters in diameter from which the three gods are believed to have emerged, are worshipped as a sanctuary in

Confucian rituals. The myth is originally a shaman song and a story of the shamanistic gods, with Confucian elements of genealogy later added. The origin of the Three-Holes seems to have been as totems of serpents, which as a form of religion served to combine clans into tribal communities. This myth seems to have existed hereditarily in the *ponp'uri* from 200 A.D. until some 600 years ago.

6. The Plot and Theme of *Ponp'uri*

The *ponp'uri* of a shrine-god is depicted above. However, the plot of the *ponp'uri* of gods in general is approximately as follows. In the prologue, the story begins with the introduction of the relationship between father and son or between husband and wife. Characters are born of a noble family as a result of the family having prayed to Buddha. They suffer many kinds of hardship, sometimes showing hostility to the upper classes. Finally, they win victory over the upper classes and live happily ever after. In the epilogue, the characters come to assume their position as gods.

Such a plot is similar to the plots of the vernacular novels of the Yi Dynasty. The theme of such novels is that of reward brought through worship of both Buddhism and shamanism.

7. The World of Gods and Hierarchy of Gods

The *ponp'uri* of a shrine-god deals with Cheju Island and with Mt. Halla as its center, the sea surrounding the island, and the mainland or the land of Dragon King across the sea. There is no heaven or world under the ground. Mt. Halla is the place where the gods emerge, hunt, and lead their lives by eating flesh. The mainland and the sea are the home of the goddesses, and from these, they enter the island. The sea is also the domain where the gods drift about displaying their heroism. The *ponp'uri* of a shrine-god is deeply rooted in the native life of the island, developed and handed down on the island.

On the other hand, the *ponp'uri* of other gods are profoundly influenced by Buddhism, and do not refer to the sea in relation to the island society. Therefore, the earth and heaven figure as the center of the gods' activities. A careful reading of the *ponp'uri* shows that the future life, or hell which is often mentioned in Buddhism, has not been

included in its conception. A realistic view of the people's needs is
connected with all the religious rites, which aim at healing diseases,
and enjoying wealth and long life. To wish that the departed souls
might live in paradise is to wish that no malignant spirits will haunt
the family descendants.

The worship of progenitors, which is strictly observed in Confucian rites, is seldom observed in shamanism. It is often said that
there are 18,000 gods, which means that shamanism is polytheistic.
These gods may be divided into three classes: gods in heaven, gods of
village-shrines, and gods of the family. When all the gods are
worshipped simultaneously, the ritual is conducted by arranging the
gods in order of importance.

III. *Ponp'uri* of the Shrine-god
and Major Forms of Worship

A. Shrine Rituals and the *Ponp'uri*

Rites are normally observed twice or four times a year by women
gathered at the shrine, and the order of observance of the rite is as
follows:

1. The invocation of spirits: by naming the place, date, and motive
for invocation, and by prayers asking the spirits to be present with
them.

2. Offering of a feast: by listing the names of the food arranged at
the altar, and by prayers asking the spirits to eat the food.

3. *Ponp'uri*: here relating the history and legend of the god to be
praised.

4. Supplication: for peace and abundance for the whole village.
After this, housewives draw near the shaman one after the other and
ask for their own respective needs, some for health and others for
wealth.

5. Divination: asking for the god's will by the use of fortune-telling
devices.

6. Entertaining the spirits: shamanism is anthropomorphic which
means that dancing and enjoying oneself and bowing down before the

spirits is the way of pleasing them.

7. Sending the spirits: when the rites are over, the spirits are asked to leave the shrine.

The above is the basic pattern of shamanistic rituals in the island. If the purpose of the rites and offerings is to exorcise the spirits of disease, the prayer is to make a boat out of straw and sail it with many offerings so that the spirits may go away on it.

B. *Iret-tang* or Seventh-day-shrine and Diseases Indigenous to the Island

According to *Iret-tang-ponp'uri* (*ponp'uri* of the Seventh-day-shrine), the daughter of the Dragon King settled at Tosanri to practise the treatment of diseases such as infantile diseases, eye diseases, skin diseases, and stomach disorders. This is not without some basis, considering the geographical location of the island. This investigator has learned from the Indigenous Diseases Research Center that since the foundation of the island is primarily rock, it is very hard to dig a deep well, and therefore, the drinking water is impure. What is worse, microfilaria, a kind of disease that is carried by mosquitoes is common on the island. The disease breaks out around coastal villages, and the number of positive cases is 58.6 percent among coastal residents. Almost 20.5 percent of the positive cases show clinical manifestations, fever, headache, other aches and pains, lumbago, lymphadenitis, lymphangitis, and haematuria. In addition, according to the Research Center Reports, 4.6 percent of the people suffer from elephantiasis, which makes one's arms and legs swell, and one's skin look like elephant's skin, and which leaves the sufferer unable to work.

C. *Yŏdŭred-dang* or Eighth-day-shrine and Snake-gods

Snake-gods are divided into two types: the snake-gods as understood in *Yŏdŭred-dang-ponp'uri* (*ponp'uri* of Eighth-day-shrine) and those in *Ch'ilsŏng-ponp'uri* or Seven-Star-ponp'uri. The snake-worship of the first type is passed on from mother to daughter in a family.

People don't like to get married to a girl belonging to such a family, because marriage with such girls, they believe, will cause the couple to worship the objectionable snake-gods.

Snake-worship on Cheju is recorded as early as 500 years ago, and the *yŏdŭret-tang* spirit is said in mythology to have come from Chŏlla-do in the southwestern part of the mainland. If one did not worship and treat the god favorably, it was believed that accidents would occur in one's family and this belief persists today. Therefore, if some accident occurs, one has to worship the snake-god right away, since such an accident is understood to have been caused by ill-treatment of the snake-god.

The snake-gods of the second type are believed to be the gods of wealth. Mythology says that the only daughter of a noble family became pregnant through the magic of a monk, and, after being thrown into the sea in a stone-basket, drifted to the island. She became a mother-snake or *bat-ch'ilsŏng* and is thought to live on a bundle of straw in the backyard. An-ch'ilsŏng is said to exist in a rice container made of earthenware which is placed in a storehouse, and worshipping it is believed to make one rich. In reality, there is no snake in the rice container, and though this belief has almost died out now, it is practised so stealthily among its remaining worshippers that it is extremely hard to investigate the practice by asking questions.

Traces of this practice can still be found on the mainland, and records of the same sort of practice appear in the *Susin'gi* of the fourth century in China. In Japan, a similar folk practice is also still observable.

D. *Yŏngdŭng-kut* and the Spirit of the Wind

There is a belief that the spirit of the wind visits the southern part of the mainland and Cheju-do between the 1st and the 15th of February. In some localities this spirit is a female, while in others it is considered male, so that we hear it referred to both as "Grandmother-Yŏngdŭng" or "Great King-Yŏngdŭng." This belief dates back about 500 years according to the available literature.

On the mainland, villagers worship it individually, while on Cheju

Island, those who are engaged in fishing worship the wind-spirit as a propagator of sea products such as seaweed, which gives us a clue to understand the oceanic character of the island culture and women's position and value there. In China, according to record, there is also a spirit of wind, and a similar folk-belief is inherited in Japan. All these folk-beliefs reflect a primitive concern for meteorology, especially for oceanic meteorology.

E. The History of Shrines and Rites

Before the Yi Dynasty, that is, in literature more than 500 years old, such communal rituals as seen above were manifested in the form of gregarious songs and dances participated in both by men and women. At present only women play a leading part in this kind of singing and dancing on the island. The reason for this split between the religious activities of men and women can be traced to the policies of the ruling group. Yi Hyungsang, governor of Cheju-do in the Yi Dynasty, in his efforts to eliminate both shamanism and Buddhism, destroyed all the temples and shrines in 1703. The primary reason for such a destructive act was that his rationalistic Confucian thought conflicted with shamanism and Buddhism. The Confucian policy of the Yi dynasty had a great influence upon the formation of the duality of Korean religious society that can be observed at the present time, a duality that was not present previously.

III. The *Ponp'uri* of General Spirits

A. Types of Ritual

When we classify the types of ritual, they may be divided into regular and non-regular ones. Regular rituals are more numerous than the latter. In larger shrines, four rites are observed annually—the New Year Rite in January, the *Yŏngdŭng*-Rite in February, the Propagation Rite for Horses and Cattle or the Rite for Cleaning Spirits' Costumes in July, and the Thanksgiving Rite in October. These are conducted communally, but there are individually observed rites at the shrines, such as Seventh-day rites.

More than half the rites observed at individual homes are performed around the 15th of January, and in the eighth and ninth month of the lunar calendar. The rites in January are for peace and abundance, while those in the eighth and ninth months are for offering thanks for a plentiful harvest.

In non-regular rites, the primary concerns are for giving birth to babies and bringing them up, and for healing diseases. Since it is believed that the spirits are in charge of all these things, the various rites must be offered to please the spirits according to their tastes.

There is also a *k'ŭn-kut* or a major-rite lasting for more than three days, in which six shamans, taking turns, worship all the spirits in order of rank, with the most important ones at the beginning.

B. The Myth of Cosmogony

At the beginning of the major-rite, *k'ŭn-kut*, the recitation of the myth begins with cosmogony, Korean history and geography, and then narrows down to the history and geography of Cheju Island. After the recitation, shamans address the spirits, "Such and such a person is offering such and such's heart and soul. Please, all the spirits, do descend upon him." This is a summoning ritual. In this, there are stories of how earth and heaven became separated, how a gigantic bird opened its wings, how two suns and two moons were created, but they battled and destroyed each other's partner so that finally only one sun and moon remained. Similar stories used to be present in the central region of the mainland and in Hamgyŏng-do province in the northeastern region. In Hmagyŏng-do, all these are supposedly done by the Buddha and Mirung, an indication of the strong influence of Buddhism. The concept of the "Enormous Bird" in such ritual appears only on Cheju Island, which gives an idea of the peculiarity of the island within the Korean sphere, since the concept of such a bird is commonly found only in Oceania. This shaman-song is called "The Establishment of Heaven and Earth."

C. The *Ponp'uri* or Myth of the Birth-Spirit

There are the *ponp'uri* of the birth-spirit, of the measles-spirit and of the smallpox-spirit. Although the latter has died out, the natives believe that measles are caused by a spirit and thus they should entreat the spirit of the disease to depart. They worship the god of birth for relief from various children's diseases. In these rituals, shamans put on make-up and do a theatrical performance in which the evil spirits of the various diseases run away in fear. Since the natives believe that the spirit of birth protects children under 15 years of age, they worship that spirit when a child is suffering from a disease, and appeal to the spirit so that a baby may be conceived and safely delivered.

D. The Myth of the Shaman-ancestors

Three brothers, the shaman's ancestors, are said to have been born of a Buddhist monk, so some shamans maintain that shamanism came from Buddhism. There is no doubt that Buddhism has had a great influence upon shamanism, but there is a similar shaman-song on the mainland where the three brothers are gods of agriculture, and gods of longevity. On Cheju Island the three brothers are said to have passed the higher civil service examination, but they failed to gain admission to the higher positions because they were sons of monks, and so they became shamans. This seems to have been a reflection of the Yi Dynasty's policy when monks were legally considered outcasts, as contrasted with the Koryŏ Dynasty which adopted Buddhism as the national religion and held monks in high esteem.

Shamans called these three ancestral brothers "Sammyŏngdu", and called their three shaman-tools Sammyŏngdu, i.e., *sinkhal* (a god's sword), *pang'ul* (a bell) and *samp'an* (divining-tools). This means that the *sammyŏngdu* is the symbol of the three ancestral brothers. These three things are used: 1) to enter into the minds of the three ancestral gods, 2) provide access to the spirits of the ancestral gods, and 3) help expedite the performance of rites. This shaman-song is called *Chogong-Ponp'uri.*

E. The *Ponp'uri* of a God Supervising the Magic-flowers in the Western Sky

This is a story about a god supervising the magic-flowers that take

charge of the life and death of human beings in the western sky. This
story is found in old Buddhist scriptures, in the shaman-songs of
north-western Pyŏngan-do province, and in the romances of the Yi
Dynasty. All these appear to have come from stories in the Buddhist
scriptures, indicating the strong Buddhist influence in the area. This is
called *Igong-ponp'uri.*

F. The Myth of a God Supervising Predestination

This myth deals with a youngest daughter who turned out to be
unfilial and yet brought her parents great fortune. The motif is of a
King Lear type and is connected with a famous legend on how temples
came into being. Shamans are made up as actresses to sing and
dramatize the story. After that, they declare that people are forced to
yield to the temptation to drink, to gamble, and to steal, even though
they do not desire to do all these evil things. They say that they are
predestined and try to drive away the temptations. This way of
thinking is Buddhist and is indicative of the many Buddhistic factors
found in the *ponp'uri.*This is called *Samgong-ponp'uri.*

G. *Segyŏng-Ponp'uri* (Myth of the Fertility-goddess)

This is one of the longest shaman-songs. The plot resembles a love
story and is similar to examples found in the Yüan, Ming and Ch'ing
dynasties in China. In Korea it began to be present in folk-tales and
romances in the Yi Dynasty, but the existence of the same kind of
shaman-songs in northeastern Hamgyŏng-do makes it hard to determine which was the original form. The Cheju-do shaman-song says
that the heroines in the story later became fertility-goddesses (*Chesŏk-
halmang* or *Śakra* in Buddhism). When people pray for an abundance
of crops, the shaman sings this *ponp'uri,* and when they perform a
major-kut, they also use it. They dramatize the following story: a
woman, fleeing from her husband's home, passes urine in the field,
where she is violated and later nurses her new-born baby conceived
during the rape scene. The audience is interested in the drama, but the
symbolic significance here is that men of primitive times often

performed sexual intercourse at the sowing season or harvest time. The story ends by saying that the son grows up to do farm-work and collects a good harvest.

H. *Ponp'uri* of Messengers

The messengers are considered to belong to the Ten Kings of the other world, who take people away from this world. Hence to die, is often expressed by the term, "to be taken away." The messengers are worshipped along with the Ten Kings when there are seriously sick persons or when a dead-spirit needs to be appeased. This comes originally from Buddhistic ideas of hells, and one can find the same myths in both Cheju-do and Hamgyŏng-do. The rites serving the Ten Kings are either performed separately or included in bigger *kut* or rites, in which they are regarded as the most important of deities.

I. Myth of the Guardian God of the House

The myth of the guardian god of the house is the end of a long story, in which the guardian god acts as husband, the goddess of fire as the legal wife, and seven sons as seven stars, or gods of the gate. The goddess of the water-closet is considered as a concubine. The gods of the gate are frequently worshipped at the beginning of the year, when every god in the house entertains another deity. The goddess of fire takes part in the meeting of the heavenly gods for seven days during the end and the beginning of a new year, a custom also found in Okinawa. These rites seem to be influenced by Chinese Taoism. The goddess of fire (the legal wife) in the kitchen and the goddess of the water-closet (the concubine) are on bad terms, so that if even a small stick from each domain should encroach on the other's territory, they are said to cause trouble. This belief may be based on a primitive knowledge of sanitation.

J. Myth of Myŏnggam or Messenger

Myŏnggam is also one of the messengers to the other world. The story says that a hunter, thinking that the messenger was going to take him away, gives a good party for him with major-rites and gets his span of life extended to forty-thousand years. This bears resemblance to Buddhist miracle tales and shows an interaction of the two religions. Myŏnggam was originally worshipped by hunters in the mountains.

K. Myth of Yŏnggam

This myth does not show any traces of Buddhistic influence, nor does it form a complete narration. Yŏnggam is the honorary title of a demon who sometimes drives an attractive woman-diver into a frenzy by inducing her to cohabit with him. When this happens, shamans perform a drama in which they play the part of his brothers who take him away in the night by the light of a torch. Yŏnggam is also regarded as a smithgod. In Siberian shamanism a smith is more respected than a shaman and it is noteworthy that Sŏkt'alhae, the Fourth King of Old Silla, was himself a smith.

Conclusion

1. Geographical Characteristics of Shamanism in Cheju Island

Shamanism in Cheju Island has been influenced by that of the mainland. It is of an archaic form and while it has its local flavour, it also includes some cultural elements of the East China Sea area.

Shaman rituals are mainly held for the purpose of obtaining a good harvest, but there are also rituals for cattle-raising at the base of Mt. Halla. These rituals have a strong oceanic characteristic.

2. Structural Characteristics of Shamanism in Cheju Island

There exist not only possessed shamans but also hereditary shamans like those of southern Korea. In general, shamanism on Cheju has a strongly hereditary character, but shamans neither leap with ecstasy nor make oracle pronouncements in the first person.

On the other hand, the village rituals consist of two forms: one is the male Confucian ritual (*p'oje*), the other is the female shamanistic ritual. Women's social position is high on Cheju Island.

3. Native Characteristics of the *Ponp'uri* of Shrine-Gods on Cheju Island

The *ponp'uri* of shrine-gods is found only on this island. Male gods, believed to have emerged from the earth, lead hunting and flesh-eating lives; female gods enter Cheju Island from the sea, and they live on rice. These elements reflect the history of cultural life of Cheju Island.

The *ponp'uri,* handed down since ancient times, has played an important role in developing our national literary arts by giving birth to novels about the common people in the Yi Dynasty and influencing the dramatic form of *P'ansori.*

Some Correlations between the Early Religions of Japan and Korea

lthough materials for the study of ancient culture are scarce in most countries, it is well known that close cultural relationships exist between Korea and Japan. For this reason, Japanese materials may be used for studies of ancient Korean culture and Korean materials are equally valuable for an understanding of the origins of Japanese culture.

One example of this is Egami Namio's theory of the "nation of horsemen." This theory attracted wide attention after World War II, suggesting as it did, that the horse-riding people of Puyŏ and Koguryŏ invaded Japan and built a country called Yamato-chotei at the beginning of the 4th century A.D. From this, there eventually emerged the country of Japan.

In Korea, a group of about ten scholars has for several years carried on research to trace the relations of ancient Japanese and Korean cultures in such fields as archaeology, history, mythology, religion, costumes, food, housing, and so on, and papers dealing with the results of their work will be published shortly in Korea and Japan. In this paper, we will attempt only to show some of the cultural relations between the two countries in the realm of religion.

We might begin by comparing the sacred regalia of both countries. According to one myth of the founding of Korea, Hwanung, the Son of Heaven, came down to the top of Mount T'ae-baek with his 3000 followers and three sacred instruments. In Japan, Ninigi, the son of heaven, came down to the top of Mount Takashio with his 300 followers and three sacred instruments. It has been argued by many scholars that these two myths show one and the same genealogy.

The three sacred regalia were a mirror, a sword, and a comma-shaped jade. However, the number and type of regalia varied in other traditions. According to the *Kojiki* and the *Nihon shoki* for instance,

Amenohiboko, a prince of the Korean Silla dynasty, came to Japan with ten treasures. These were of four kinds: 2 mirrors, 1 sword, 4 jades, and 3 *hire* (shawls for women). It is held that these precious and important sacred regalia were preserved in the shrine of Isenokami and in Yamato-chotei. Another example is the *Kogosuyi* (807 A.D.) which states that only the Sword and the Mirror were magical implements for self- protection. It appears, therefore, that originally, the sacred regalia were either of two or of four kinds, but that after the ninth century, only three kinds of sacred regalia were recognized.

Little is known about the three sacred regalia in the Korean myth, since there remains no written record of them. Ch'oe Nam-sŏn has argued that the three sacred regalia might have been a mirror, a sword and a crown, although a bell, or a drum, could have been included instead of a crown.

As indicated above, two of the three—the mirror and the sword—are found in both the Korean and the Japanese myths. According to most records, the sacred regalia used in Japan came from Korea, and the Japanese myth shows the same structure and genealogy as the Korean myth.

Another form of comparison is archeological. In this case, it is clear that during the bronze age, certain ritual implements began to be used; that is, at the latest, during the sixth century B.C.

The sacred implements of the bronze age in Korea were swords, mirrors and bells and these items show more delicate craftsmanship than do the present-day Shaman instruments. Research has shown that some of the swords were not sharpened, and hence, must have been used for ritual, and also that the area of their distribution covered southwestern Manchuria, the Korean Peninsula and western Japan. In this entire area, the characteristics of the artifacts are similar, so that it is assumed that close cultural relations existed. An example of the similarities is seen in the fact that the mirrors had two knobs on their backs, and are called double-knobbed mirrors in contrast to Chinese bronze-age mirrors, which usually had only one knob. It is assumed that these bronze implements were transmitted to Japan through Korea during the Yayoi period (about 300 B.C. - 300 A.D.), and the area of distribution is known to cover western Japan, northern Kyushu and the Kinki district. However, the distribution, the use, and the actual dating of these artifacts are complicated and only a skilled archeologist can deal adequately with their complexity. Perhaps enough has been said here to at least indicate their similarities and their possible relationships.

A third area of comparision is that of folklore. Swords, mirrors and bells are still used in shaman rituals which have been preserved in Korea. The *myŏngdu,* for instance, the modern version of a bronze mirror, is passed down from a master-shaman to his chief disciple when the master-shaman dies. The *myŏngdu* is regarded as the soul, or the symbol, of the master. Similarly, at many shaman rituals, the shaman sings and dances with her sword and bell in her hands.

Similar phenomena are also found in Japan. A metal mirror is often kept in a shrine as the symbol of a god, and the priestess or shaman there often uses a sword and a bell, dancing and singing at her ritual. There is usually a large bell at the entrance to her shrine.

It is difficult to develop a full argument relating the three ancient regalia to the bronze-age ritual implements, or to the present-day Shamanistic regalia, but it seems likely that they were closely connected with each other in most parts of East Asia, particularly in Japan and Korea. It should be noted that these sacred regalia have a history of at least 3000 years, from the earliest period of Korean history, as important relgious symbols.

In court rituals there were also similarities between Korea and Japan, and it now seems well-established that in both societies, many court rituals had their origins in agricultural ceremonials, as for example the enthronement rituals.

Tŏng-mang, which has been the Korean version of Thanksgiving Day since the Koguryŏ period (37 B.C.-668 A.D.), was succeeded by the festival of *P'algwanhoe* during the Koryŏ dynasty (918-1392 A.D.). In the year in which he was crowned, a new king presided in person as master of the *P'algwanhoe* ritual.

The Japanese *Daishosai* is regarded as the same as the Korean *P'algwanhoe,* while the Japanese Thanksgiving Day is *Niinamesai.*

However, in the year in which a new ruler was enthroned, this festival was also called *Daishosai*. Since the Korean *P'algwanhoe* was abandoned because the Yi Dynasty preferred Confucian policies and rituals, the materials for an examination of *P'algwanhoe* are scarce. It is very difficult, therefore, to make a detailed comparison of it with the Japanese *Daishosai*. It is not difficult, however, to trace its origin, since it has been established that *Daishosai* was the Japanese version of shaman initiation rituals characteristic of northeastern Asia.

In Siberia, for example, a shaman candidate, in order to become a shaman, had to be wrapped in felt and then awakened from an ecstatic and seemingly dying condition. This was the symbolic procedure by which a non-sacred layman became a sacred priest. The ritual for the king's enthronement thus seems to have been developed from this rebirth ritual of Siberia. Several such examples are to be found in northeast Asia: Turkestan, Laio, Senbi, Kaya and Japan.

The procedures of the Japanese *Daishosai* ritual are very complicated, but the core of *Daishosai* seems to be the rebirth ritual of a new ruler. The procedure by which a layman is changed into a sacred ruler is as follows: the candidate lies down on the eight-pile *tatami* covered with a blanket. He lies there for an hour completely secluded from all social intercourse, symbolically removed from the world. There is general agreement among scholars that this ritual was passed down from earliest primitive times; it is also said to reflect the myth of Ninigi, the heavenly son, who came down from heaven wrapped in a blanket.

Hori Masao compared this with the myth of King Suro, of the Korean state of Kaya, as follows:

> Eggs wrapped in red cloth came down from the heavens to Mount Kuji. The chiefs of the tribes put them on a bed and, after several days, King Suro was born from one of the eggs.

Hori claims that the red cloth and the bed correspond to the Japanese blanket and the eight-pile *tatami*, respectively, were symbolic tools which would bring the sacred spirits to mankind on the earth. Hori emphasized that a close relationship existed between the myth of King

Suro and the Japanese myth.

To sum up, the *P'algwanhoe* of Koryŏ and *Niinamesai* and *Daishosai* of Japan, which were agricultural rituals for a very long time, were eventually elevated into court rituals. *P'algwanhoe* was a king's enthronement ceremony and it seems clear that the enthronement rituals of northeast Asia which influenced Korea and Japan were inherited from shaman initiation rituals.

There are two final comparisons to be made. The first of these is the form given to shrines in both countries. It has been often claimed that the Japanese term for shrine (*jingu*) originated in Korea during the Silla Dynasty, in the latter part of the 6th century, and was first used for the great shrine at Ise (*Ise-jingu*). No one, however, has carried out a comparative study of Korean and Japanese shrines, because little or nothing is known about early Korean shrines. An examination of the Japanese *torii*, and its Korean parallel might be useful in this regard, and artifacts recently excavated in Korea and in Japan are very promising materials for future research.

It should be noted, first of all, that there is considerable controversy concerning the origin of the *torii*.Is it of Japanese origin, or Chinese, or of northeastern Asia, or Indian? Goto Shuichi pointed out that similar features of *torii* in house gates could be found in Manchuria and in Korea, and that in both of these places birds, carved in wood, are to be found on the top of gates. Since the term, *torii*, (which means 'birds exist') is regarded as originating from the birds on the gates, he also suggested that similar bird-like shapes found at the entrance gates of Korean rulers' tombs, or on the *hŏngsalmun*, or village entrance gates were related. Goto thus became a leading proponent of the northeastern theory of origin.

As mentioned above, about ten years ago, archaeologists working in Japan and Korea discovered some very similar artifacts. In Japan they discovered two bird-shaped wood carvings which are assumed to have come from the Yayoi Period (3rd century B.C.-3rd century A.D.). Those which were discovered in Korea show two birds engraved on one side, and are regarded as belonging to the bronze age (ca. 7th century B.C.) used as ritual tools.

It was not until much later, the late 8th century A.D., that the term *"torii"* was first found in the literature of Japan. At this time, *torii* in Japan seem to have assumed the present-day form, characterized as follows:

1. a straw rope, twisted to the left, is hung on the *torii,* at the shrine ritual;
2. the straw rope is regarded as the boundary of the shrine;
3. in rural areas, a stone is customarily put on the *torii* to symbolize good luck;
4. no bird shape is discernible at present, but *torii* still means that 'a bird exists';
5. the *torii* itself symbolizes sacredness.

In Korean folk-custom, there is a long tradition of the *sottae.* This is a long pole on the top of which a bird, carved in wood, is put. It may stand alone at the entrance to a village, or be placed together with a man also carved in wood. Depictions on early bronzes, however, indicate that it was usually set up alone. The Korean *sottae,* together with the *jang-sŭng,* or man carved in wood, also shows five characteristics as follows:

1. a straw rope twisted to the left is hung on the *sottae* at rituals of a village;
2. the rope is the boundary of the village. The *sottae* and *jang-sŭng* protect the village from the invasion of evil spirits.
3. When anyone passes these objects they customarily throw stones at them;
4. wood carvings of birds are put on the top of long poles;
5. *Sottae* and *jang-sŭng* are symbols of sacredness and the objects of worship.

In summary: the close relations between *torii* and *sottae* are clearly apparent. It should be noted, however, that in Korea, *sottae* have been suppressed for more than five hundred years and regarded as superstition, due largely to the influence of Confucian concepts and beliefs. On the other hand, *torii* in Japan became a symbol of national

Shinto and continued to undergo changes and development. It is difficult, because of these changes, to determine its origin with any degree of accuracy.

Our final comparision concerns the form of ritual worship. A common perception of scholars of religion is that the content of most religious rituals may be divided into two parts: *legomenon* (singing) and *dromenon* (action). J. Harrison has pointed out that *'dromenon'* and *'drama'* had the same meaning in ancient Greece and that ancient rituals had a close relationship with ancient arts. This may be diagrammed as follows:

             legomenon   . . . (*p'uri*)

ritual

           dromenon (drama)   . . . (*nori*)

In Korea, the term *sŏngju-p'uri* means "rite of a house god", and has two aspects—song and ritual. According to Japanese scholars, *p'uri* is regarded as having the same origin as the Japanese *puri*, or *furi*, which refer to 'ritual song' or simply 'ritual' in local dialects, such as those of Kyushu. These same words are also found in Japanese medieval literature, and in Okinawa. The term *'p'uri'* is said to mean 'harvest ritual' or 'rich harvest ritual'. Some scholars claim that the Japanese *puri*, or *furi*, have the same origin as the Korean *p'uri*.

The term *'nori'* in Korean is a nominal form of the Korean verb *nol-da*. There is also the phrase *'tae-gam nori'* which means 'fortune-god ritual'. It is claimed that money can be made by anyone who pleases the fortune-god at his ritual. At this ritual, a shaman possessed by the fortune god sings, dances and delivers oracles of the fortune god.

There is a similar term, *'norito'*, in Japanese, but its origin and meaning are not clear. Some scholars claim that *'norito'* may mean 'oracles of a god delivered by an officiating priest possessed by a god'. It is also speculated that *'nori'* has the meaning of 'oracle', and that *'to'* may come from the word *kotoba* (language), or *tokoro* (place). The meaning of *norito* is thus not clear, but as shown above, the Korean *nori* and the Japanese *norito* have a similar meaning: "a god's words".

When it is recalled that the Korean *p'uri* and the Japanese *'puri'* have the same origin and meaning in connection with *legomenon,* one of the two parts in a religious ritual, it seems likely that the Korean *'nori'* can be related to the Japanese *'norito'* and that both are related to the remaining part of a religious ritual, the *dromenon.*

In ancient Japanese literature, many magico-religious elements are to be found in the priests' hymns. The same is also true in Korean shamanism. The contents of rituals in both countries are similar, as shown above in both *legomenon (p'uri)* and *dromenon (nori* and *norito).*

In conclusion, we might recapitulate our findings that the relations between Japan and Korea in the matter of religion seem to have been very close indeed. Even closer relationships can be found in neighboring fields of study such as archaeology, mythology, food, costume, architecture, etc. These, of course, constitute only a portion of Japanese culture, not the whole of it. It should also be noted that in different periods of its history, Japan imported a variety of different cultural aspects from the outside world. Even though some aspects of Korean culture were imported to Japan, the Japanese assimilated and changed whatever they took over.

In Korea, when Confucianism became the state ideology during the Yi dynasty, shamanism was actively suppressed, being regarded as superstition, although it still has strong ties and support among the population. It is generally conceded that the social realization of Confucianism was much stronger in Korea than in China, and that even in the present-day life of Koreans, worship of ancestors, filial piety, and morality between men and women are remarkable. It is often said that Korean ethics are characterized by blood relatedness, and are sectarian in character; in other words, they are vertical ethics.

In contrast to this, Japanese culture is said to be territorial and a culture of solidarity. Shintō seems to show one such aspect with its festivals or *matsuri* symbolizing territorial solidarity. Thus, even though close relations exist between Korea and Japan in the area of religion, there are considerable differences in other cultural characteristics between the two countries.

Shamanism and the
Korean World-view

═══════════

I. Family and Life-Cycle

The philosophical views and cultic rituals known as shamanism have exercised a profound influence on the development of Korean attitudes and practices. Because shamanism is Korea's earliest and only indigenous religion, its influence pervades many aspects of Korean life and, in some instances, rivals that of the major world religions which were imported at a later date. This essay focuses on the pattern of culutral perspectives which have been closely identified with Korean shamanism, with emphasis on the ways in which this world-view has manifested itself in the daily lives of Koreans. Part one of the essay will consider those values and practices which are most directly concerned with the individual, his life, and his family. In part two, we will take up some of the wider social, political, and religious consequences of the shamanistic world-view.

Korean shamanism has undergone prolonged and intensive interaction with four religions: Buddhism, Confucianism, Taoism, and Christianity. For this reason, the world-view discussed in this article cannot be considered a 'purely' shamanistic view; no attempt has been made to isolate the primordial shamanistic world-view from those modifications or accretions which have resulted from its interaction with other cultural perspectives. Indeed, one of the reasons Korean shamanism has been able to survive has been the facility with which it intertwined with other, often less tolerant, religions.

A Godless World

Many of the fundamental assumptions of Western culture have no counterparts in the world-view of Korean shamanism. The shamanistic world-view, for instance, posits no god at—or as—the center of the universe. Human existence is not thought to be assigned meaning by a transcendent abstract, or omnipotent being who has created the universe and now guides its history. Life is not understood to be a unidirectional linear progression with a clear beginning and end, nor is history considered a series of stages in the "development" of human perfection.

In the view of Korean shamanism, human beings come into the world as integral parts of the rhythm of nature. But an individual does not come from another world at birth, nor does he leave this world when he dies. Rather, each person has been in this world since the beginning of life and remains here after death. Man is so closely intertwined with the terrestrial forces of nature, in fact, that man without nature would be impossible and nature without man inconceivably irrelevant. Man lives in and with nature, and has with it a relationship which is neither amicable nor antagonistic. The shamanistic man does not fear annihilation by nature, and thus does not consider it necessary to dominate it; man can no more subjugate nature than can nature have dominion over man. Since there is no god to "put all things under man's feet," the shamanistic man lives best by flowing with the rhythm of nature. This is not to say, however, that the shamanistic man lives in "perfect harmony" with nature, nor that he is an abject slave to its rhythms. Man is under no obligation to freeze to death in a harsh winter merely for the sake of harmony with nature. He builds a fire and a warm shelter, clothes homself warmly and nourishes himself with meat. The bitter cold of winter is not an expression of the enmity of nature, nor are the earthquakes, floods, and fierce animals which threaten man. All are part of the balance maintained by nature. Every form of life, including human life, will be sustained if it manages to adapt its life style to the rhythm and balance of nature.

In correspondence with the overall balance and rhythm of nature, man attains the fullest life by becoming as completely "human" as possible. Although the mythology and history of other cultures detail the stories of heroes said to be of divine origin, in Korean shamanism even the heroes are thoroughly human. For the shamanistic man,

perfection does not consist of obedience to divine commands, nor of
godliness and divinity—which he considers dehumanized, nonhuman
conditions. Since he has no god who encumbers his life with demands
for absolute perfection, the shamanistic man never feels that his life
has become an endless sequence of foibles and failures. And, since he
acknowledges no transcendent state of human existence, this-worldly
existence is the only one that matters. Life in this world is too precious
to be a mere preparatory transition to a more perfect and permanent
life in another (nonhuman) dimension of existence. Other-worldly
existence in a nonhuman dimension is, by definition, irrelevant.

In keeping with his emphasis on attaining a fully "human"
condition, the shamanistic man acknowledges no hierarchy of human
faculties. *Logos* or reason is not considered "closer to god", nor are
human instincts denigrated as flawed by original sin. The shamanistic
man fails to be enchanted by the dichotomy of spirit against body, and
the notion that one is somehow superior to the other is as alien to him
as the idea that the two are hostile to each other. Since the shamanistic
man does not think in terms of a dualism of man and god, he is free of
dualistic obsessions in other aspects of his thought. Thus, just as man
and nature form a mutually overlapping continuum, all human
features and faculties are essential to the make-up of an individual.

Although the shamanistic man recognizes human faculties such as
intelligence, wisdom, logic, reason, mind, spirit, soul, and so forth,
these are inseparable from the overall biological process—particularly
the senses. As keen hearing and clear sight make quick intelligence, a
sound mind cannot be detached from a sound body. Indeed, a
disembodied soul is inhuman, and therefore usually inimical to
humanity. To the shamanistic man, the human soul and body are not
discrete and separable. They constitute a continuum, a mutually
overlapping, interpenetrating, and conjunctive whole.

Marriage and Procreation

In Korean shamanism, marriage has never been merely the union
of two individuals; it is, rather, the marriage of one family to another.
Although the compatability of the prospective bride and bridegroom

were taken into account, marriages were usually arranged by senior members of the family who had evaluated several promising families with which they shared common values and life style. In ancient Korea, betrothals and marriages took place early in order to ensure the continuation of the bloodline: girls were usually about fifteen when they married, and boys were usually younger. In most cases, the bride and bridegroom had never met before their wedding. Although the practice of "arranged" weddings has remained in modern Korea, some modifications have been made. Now, the usual practice is for the young to be introduced by a go-between after a preliminary clearance and approval by their respective families. After several "dates", if the youngsters find each other acceptable, then the betrothal and wedding take place.

Of all the acts which contribute to the attainment of a fully "human" condition, the union of a man and woman to create a new life is most significant. Through it, they enlarge not only their own lives, but also life itself. Although sexual morality has traditionally been very rigid in Korea—owing to the influence of Confucianism—the under-lying shamanistic view of sex has exercised a tempering influence. If there were "natural rights" for the shamanistic person, the right to sex would be one of them. For a man to be thoroughly male and a woman thoroughly female, in a biological sense, is to be in full agreement with the rhythm of nature. Just as summer is naturally hot and winter naturally cold, both man and woman are equally indispensable and productive; neither is superior to the other.

Korean shamanism has never viewed the relations between the two sexes as a perpetual struggle. It is neither possible nor necessary for one sex to dominate the other, since both must be complementary if new life is to be created. If either sex has the right to boast of being more productive, it is the female. But although she is endowed with the appropriate biological structure to shoulder the larger share of reproduction and nurture of progeny, the male has as much stake in the successful fulfillment of this creative process. He has an obligation to himself, if not to the female and the child, to do everyting in his power to assist in child-rearing. Philosophers in other cultures have theorized that dialectical tension between opposing forces provides the motive power for progress. Sexual dialectics have also been included in this paradigm, in which productive power is supposed to arise from the dialectical opposition of the two sexes. Shamanistic dialectics, however, reaffirms the existential continuum between the two sexes. They are not opposing forces, but mutually attracting incomplete forces (or halves), waiting to be complemented and completed. Through the sexual union, the egos overlap and interlock. Now, the pain of the one is the pain of the other; the death of one is the partial death of the other.

Although Korean shamanism considers sex-roles to have been biologically defined and ordained, the value which is placed upon them differs greatly from that common in Western culture. Since the reproduction of human life is considered a heroic act, for instance, men have no monopoly on heroism. And, since no premium has been attached to the ability to reason in the abstract or to artistic creativity, the "mere" reproduction of human beings has never been considered demeaning drudgery devised to enslave women. Shamanistic persons can see why women in more militaristic cultures might feel mistreated; if society bestows prestige and honor upon those who derive power and wealth from the capability to destroy human life efficiently, women become mere prizes of war. In such a society, it is the talent to destroy life rather than the capacity to procreate that is esteemed and revered.

Shamanism has never approved of homosexuality. And yet, it does not condemn homosexuality as a sin or crime deserving of eternal damnation. Homosexuality is regarded as a temporary aberration to which a human-being may be driven when deprived of heterosexual opportunities for a protracted period of time. Shamanism also accepts the fact that the intensity of sexuality differs among people. Some may have less enthusiasm for life and its enlargement than others, and there may be those who would rather engage in unprocreative sex. In the shamanistic view, life is diverse enough to accommodate those who disdain human reproduction; after all, *continua* exist in morality as well as in sexuality.

The death of the Husband often resulted in real suffering for the wife. Inasmuch as remarriage was prohibited by Confucian ethics, a childless young widow was often compelled to finish her life without any opportunity to bear her own child. While the family line of her deceased husband could be easily continued through adoption, the wife's personal fulfillment was impossible. The harsh rigidity of Confucian discipline was circumvented by a consensual abduction for clandestine elopement coupled with a fake suicide. These subterfuges were employed to meet the shamanistic demand to alleviate the anguish of the childless widow while saving the Confucian respectability of both families of the marriage.

Kinship and Blood Ties

Of all interpersonal relations, none has more warmth than kinship. As a person's existence begins with other human beings, kinship becomes the foundation and most convincing affirmation of life. To the shamanistic man, a man without a family is a most wretched human being; even his humanity is suspect. Kinship gives meaning to life, protects one from loneliness, and is the best assurance of one's humanity.

Because Korean shamanism views kinship as a biological continuum which extends from the beginning of life into the future, the shamanistic man achieves a sort of immortality by ensuring the continuity of his bloodline. There is a biological overlap between a child and its parents; just as a part of the parents exists in the child, a part of the child exists in the parents. In the shamanistic view, this means that a part of the child has existed in all of its forebears since the beginning of life. Herein lies the empirical reason for the tremendous importance which the shamanistic man attaches to blood ties.

To a shamanistic man, a child of his own blood possesses a "religious" significance: a child revitalizes and confirms the existence of all its forebears and relations. Since the child is a part of the existential continuum of the family, its ego overlaps with those of the parents and other close kindred; there is no clear-cut ego boundary.

The extent of this ego-overlap varies according to the proximity of the blood ties; parents are the closest, with diminishing overlap in the case of more distant relatives. Egos that are not related, however, may also come to be closely linked through friendship or other forms of interpersonal relationship, and these are frequently likened to the ego-overlap which pertains to relatives. One who develops close interpersonal relations with others is respected for his decency and humanity, while one who is reluctant to "give his inside" to others is considered to be of small humanity.

The close ego ties which link the shamanistic parents to their children present a striking contrast to most Western cultures, in which a child's autonomy and self-sufficiency are considered minimum requirements for mental health. In Western culture, parents who fail to consider their child to be a separate and discrete ego become classic examples of serious mental illness. They are certain to ruin their child's chances to become productive and vital in society. The stress in child rearing is on the inculcation, as early as possible, of the sense of autonomy and separate identity.

The shamanistic parent is deeply baffled by such an approach to parenthood, since in his relationship to his child there is no need for projection or for psychological identification; the ego-overlap of parent and child is so thorough that autonomy is not considered a virtue.

Shamanistic parents keep their child in constant bodily contact. In early infancy, the mother provides this contact, and the father substitutes whenever the mother is unavailable. In situations where neither parent is available, the bodily warmth of some human being is still considered essential for the healthy development of the child. Constant interaction with humans is thought to increase a child's humanity. The shamanistic child has little reason to feel in conflict with its environment. The "dialectical tension" between itself as subject and others as object is not emphasized, and is not considered essential for the sound personality development of the child.

Shamanism has failed to be impressed by the intrusion of sexuality into the parent-child relationship. The fact that a child is in constant contact with the mother appears to prevent the kind of childish resentment described by Freud. As both parents sleep in the same room with children of both sexes until they reach puberty, a child has little reason to feel anger against either parent for depriving it of the comforting touch and presence of the other. Intimacy and physical contact between parents and children seems to forestall any sexual insinuation. The shamanistic parent-child relationship may be simply too close, affectionate, and full of bodily contact to admit of any Freudian suggestions.

To a dualistic mind, the child-rearing practices of Korean shamanistic parents spells disaster by breeding an unhealthy "dependency mentality" in the child and causing a basic confusion in epistemology— a confusion of the ego with the nonego. But in order to have "dependency," there must first be a dichotomy of the dependent-subject and the dependee-object as separate and discrete entities. Where egos overlap and interlock, however, there may be interpenetration and existential continuum, but no dependency. The shamanistic person would find a life in which egos are all autonomous, separate, discrete, and self-sufficient too cold, impersonal, lonely, and inhuman. It should be noted, however,that the overlap of egos in shamanistic culture does not signify a merger or fusion of egos. Rather, the overlapping egos interpenetrate one another, forming a commonly shared area, while leaving the remainder different and distinct. The resulting condition is neither a single ego nor two discrete egos, but something indeterminate which can only be described as something more than one but less than two. Nor is there any resultant epistemological confusion; the parent always remains parent, and child always remains child. Even death does not alter these relations: if there is anything permanent and eternal for a shamanistic person, it is the interpersonal relations formed and maintained during his lifetime.

In Korea every interpersonal relation—whether characterized by positive or negative emotion—is so intense that two strangers often find it extremely difficult to establish an impersonal, yet minimally civil, arm's-length relationship. It is nearly impossible for a shamanistic person to develop and maintain a personal relationship without emotional involvement. A relationship without an ego-overlap would be unnatural and inhuman. For this reason, when two strangers must interact with one another, an introduction by a third party is customarily required. This introduction provides an instant ego-overlap. The quality and extent of initial ego-overlap are determined by the nature of the relationship which already exists between the respective parties and the introducer, as well as by the latter's "humanity" as recognized by the community at large. Where third-party introduction is not available, each stranger begins by giving his biographical data in detail, with the objective of discovering some point of ego-overlap—however tenuous or indirect—hitherto unknown to them. Given the ethnic homogeneity of Korea and its comparatively small size, any two individuals usually manage to find some common acquaintance or local ties on which to base their relationship.

Humanity, Emotion, and Ethics

As we have already noted, to the shamanistic man, the fullest life is one in which the individual becomes as fully "human" as possible. This same attitude is found in the intricate structure of ethics developed by shamanistic culture. In general, that behavior which is most "human" is judged to be good, and that which is inhuman is considered evil. Just as a good life is one which is infused with human affection, an individual is considered good when he contributes to making others' lives long and joyful. In shamanistic mythology, heroes are those who excel in personal affection, enrichment of life, and productivity.

The conclusive affirmation of human existence is to be found in the sensory verification of interaction with other human beings. The fact that one can share touches, smells, sounds, sights, and tastes with other human beings becomes the strongest confirmation of one's life. Man is truly human only when he is interacting with other beings. A man who is alone and isolated from other human beings becomes less than human; the deterioration of his humanity advances as the duration and degree of isolation increases. Thus, loneliness becomes the ultimate evil and pain; it is a condition to be avoided at any cost. Even negative emotions such as anger, hatred, and jealousy are to be preferred to the total deprivation of affection, since with them there is, at least, some form of contact with other humans.

Because loneliness and isolation are so greatly feared, ostracism is a most potent and effective punishment for antisocial behavior in Korea. Exclusion from the communal network of human interaction is the pain inflicted upon the wrongdoer; banishment from home removes the solace of kinship and communal affection. Historically, the more reprehensible the crime, the greater the distance an exile would be required to travel from home. The lot of the stranger has always been woeful in Korea; he has been automatically suspect as a malefactor in exile. As a result, it was very difficult for a stranger to secure acceptance into a community as a full-fledged new member. Under such conditions, few persons would willingly depart from their familiar and comfortable homes, and this reluctance in the past has contributed to the closeness of communal ties and very low incidence of mobility among Koreans.

In preference to the deprivation of loneliness, the shamanistic man approves of the display of emotions. A strong display of emotion signifies strong humanity. So long as the emotion is not displayed for merely selfish reasons, there is no communal disapprobation of any person's display. Indeed, a man without tears is considered cold and inhuman, and even the law and justice are still called upon "to shed tears." As the essence of humanity, emotion is considered by the shamanistic man to have a powerful influence over man and nature. A monarch, however absolute, rarely dared to ignore the tearful remonstrances of his ministers, and strong negative emotions are still considered capable of playing havoc with the rhythm of nature. The common saying that the "agonizing grief of a wronged woman can bring forth frost in midsummer" indicates the strength of the belief that if a person desires something desperately enough, the sheer force of powerful emotions can bring it about.

The powerful influence of emotion has helped to inhibit crimes against individuals in Korea, since one who contemplates harming another human being must reckon with the strong negative emotions of the intended victim. In Korean shamanism, the dead are thought to be able to mobilize the forces of nature in order to exact revenge. Thus, retribution is certain; vengeance belongs to the victim and his relatives. To be sure, there may be a time-lag in revenge: actual retaliation may be visited upon the children or other loved ones of the evildoer in the manner and at the time of the victim's choice. In view of the religious significance a child has to the shamanistic man, a vengeance visited upon a child is even more greatly dreaded than one exacted from the evildoer himself. The shamanistic man is fearful of curses. But these are not understood to be invocations of suprahuman force; they are, rather, human commitments to a course of action impelled by strong emotion. In other cultures, a person may be driven to homocide because of overpowering animosity. The shamanistic man may experience a similar urge, but to slay his foe would only compound his difficulty by making him liable to reprisal from the dead nemesis. His last alternative is to commit suicide at the gate of his tormentor's house, being careful, of course, to carry a document which specifies all his woes and sufferings and enumerates the particulars of his curse. It would be a hard man, indeed, who could resist the urge to rush to make amends with the surviving members of the dead man's family.

Suicide

In view of the powerful attachment to life in Korea, taking one's own life to protest injustice naturally carries a tremendous impact on public opinion. Beyond the terrifying aspects of self-immolation as regards the individual, such an event also threatens to disrupt the natural rhythm of communal life to such an extent that the entire community is compelled to join in the effort to avenge the dead man. This explains why, when Korea was invaded by a neighboring power, many prominent Koreans committed suicide, leaving wills in which the brutal injustice was denounced. Observers of the Korean scene from more militaristic cultures have frequently criticized these self-immolations as indicative of the effeminate impotence of Korean political culture. According to such critics, it would have been more "manly" and effective to have killed as many of the invaders as possible, but such criticism shows little understanding of the emotional and shamanistic bases of the suicides.

As we have already noted, for the shamanistic man, the foreboding of loneliness is a more effective sanction than guilt. Shame, the emotional reaction felt in the face of negative reaction from the community caused by apprehension of withdrawal of personal affection is, therefore, a particularly powerful emotion for the shamanistic man. Impending ostracism is much more distressing than fear of transcendent retribution imposed by an abstract divinity as punishment for having violated a set of rigid metaphysical commandments. Indeed, the shamanistic man would hardly acknowledge the violation of such commandments to be wrong; to him, only tangible injuries to human beings can be considered evil. To be sure, violation of property rights are evil, but they are considered less culpable than emotional or bodily harm because they affect the human being less directly. The real harm in property offenses is the extent of personal pain which they cause, and their culpability is usually measured accordingly.

Shamanistic ethics are relative and situational; no attempt is made to judge human conduct according to an absolute standard. Every deed is evaluated in light of the particular equities involved and in the context of the appropriate interpersonal dynamics. A wrong in one situation need not be a wrong in another. As in all shamanistic thought, dualism is refused in shamanistic ethics also. Good and evil are taken as a continuum, comprising an overlapping and inter-penetrating whole. Neither can exist without the other, and neither is more potent or dominant than the other. Shamanistic man does not feel compelled to "wield the sword of justice" in order to destroy evil. Indeed, extirpation of evil—though practically impossible in any event—would itself be extremely evil—that is, inhuman. The shaman-istic man is always struck by the Christian symbolism of the death of Christ, since the ultimate evil of Judas' betrayal and the cruel murder of Jesus engendered the gospel of perfect love, resurrection, and salvation.

Honesty

Honesty, as an ethical quality which is characterized by stead-fastness and constancy in interpersonal affection, is highly valued by

Korean shamanism. Honesty is cherished because it requires one to be loyal to one's existential commitment to other human beings. But, as a moral attribute which compels one to tell the truth always, the shamanistic man refuses to esteem honesty as a cardinal virtue. His difficulty with this second approach lies primarily in the realization that man is incapable of knowing the truth outside a particular context. A person may know through experience a few fragmentary and disconnected facets of a situation, but such an accidental exposure to a fragmentary and disjointed sensory perception can hardly be considered the truth. Since no man knows the complete truth, and since there is no absolute god to piece together all the fragments of human perception into a whole truth, truth becomes relative and must be qualified by the particular equities of any given situation.

The shamanistic man insists that a public statement of fact ought to be evaluated in light of its specific impact upon concrete interpersonal dynamics. Every person must weigh the benefit and injury his version of the truth may produce upon those with whom he maintains interpersonal affection. The shamanistic man refuses to tell the truth if it hurts his loved ones. Indeed a man who risks pain or death by refusing to tell the truth in order to shield others is not considered a wicked liar, but a truly good and just man. By the same token, such a man would calmly accept horrible torture and death by telling the truth if his interpersonal commitment to another required this. Distortion of the truth for selfish gain is most severely condemned as vicious and despicable, but dishonesty to save a human life is not at all reprehensible. Again, a calculation of ethical gains and losses is involved. This calculation is avowedly prejudiced in favor of the interpersonal, the particular, and the tangible and against the abstract, the universal, and the ideal.

Continuum

In shamanistic thought, the continuum of the human ego is not limited to interpersonal relations and human behavior; the human ego overlaps with nonhuman beings as well. A continuum exists with everything in nature. All the parts of man's environment are necessary for his survival, and man shares his existence with nature as an inseparable part of his being. This close feeling for nature, however, has not caused the shamanistic man to anthropomorphize other life forms or natural objects. His perspective toward them has been akin to companionship or solidarity nurtured by membership and participation in a common existential venture—that is, life.

Koreans believe that every life saved and prolonged also saves and prolongs the life of the human responsible for the good deed. They often buy birds, fish, and turtles in captivity and release them with the expectation that such a deed will redound to their own benefit. This reverence for life, however, is not absolute or abstract; it is unabashedly self-protective and practical. Conservation of the food supply, for instance, impels fishing villages to hold periodic *kut* [seances] in which the fish are "revered" so that the fishermen may continue to have abundant catches. Although such "reverence" for the prey by the predator may seem self-serving, to the shamanistic mind, it is quite logical. Shamanistic folklore abounds with stories in which various species of beasts reciprocate human kindness. Simple gestures of mercy towards these beings are said to elicit responses in which they give their lives to promote the safety and welfare of humans. Moreover, the affection and charity of one human toward another is thought to have moved creatures to reward the human-hearted person. A daughter who sacrifices her life to restore sight to her blind father, for instance, is in turn saved through the help of marine creatures and vegetation.

Such negative emotions as ruthlessness and the desire for revenge, on the other hand, are said to give rise to natural disasters. It is said that when a severe drought refused to abate, the royal household attempted to mollify the natural forces by removing the bases for any negative emotions among humans and nonhumans which might have been prolonging the drought: the entire household abstained from meat, music, and dance, and prisoners were released or their death penalties commuted. It is his belief in the ego continuum that enables the shamanistic man to move other life forms, inorganic objects, and the forces of nature.

Just as the biological continuum takes a person's life beyond his birth and death, the shamanistic man views time itself as a continuum. He is reluctant to segment time into such clearly defined portions as the past, present, and future. Instead of a unidirectional linear dimension, time is understood to be a combined mixture of change and repetition. Since the rhythm of life is both changing and repeating, and since past, present, and future all contain aspects of one another, the segmentation of time into three discrete parts would be an over-simplification. In any case, the shamanistic man has seldom felt the urge to speculate metaphysically about time. Time always exists; it is man that touches it briefly and is absorbed by it. Nevertheless, time has always been missed and regretted in Korea. In their poems, songs, and ballads, Koreans have expressed the desire to tie it to a willow branch, frighten it into stopping in its tracks, plead with it to stay, trick it into slowing down, and even seduce it into spending the night. But the inexorable flow of time is also an affirmation of life. It is death that stops—or at least slows—the flight of time; in death, time becomes irrelevant. Where there is life, there is time also.

The shamanistic man's ambivalence toward time is merely a facet of his more general ambivalence toward life itself. Although he acknowledges that life can only have meaning if there is death, the shamanistic man's attachment to life makes him regret the passage of time. This ambivalence has imparted a general air of gloom to the shamanistic view of the young and the new. Unlike those in more dynamic and exuberant cultures, Koreans have been indisposed to adore youth and newness. The firm conviction that what is new must be better than what is old is lacking in shamanism. In some cultures, the word "new" is synonymous with freshness, innovation, youth, modernity, and creativity. There is a strong cultural commitment to—and faith in—change, progress, improvement, and development. And, despite some theoretical challenges to belief in the inevitability of human progress, it has remained a major premise of most mono-theistic world-views. Lacking a similar belief, Korean shamanism has been diffident about the dichotomies of progress and regress, de-velopment and decay, new and old. For the shamanistic man, newness is an extension of age, just as the future is an extension of the past and present. Nothing in human life can be totally new, having no connection whatever with the old and existent. Thus, a continuum exists which links the new and the old. The shamanistic man lacks the restless dynamism which might drive him to make a radical departure from the old for the sake of progress and development. To him, change, difference, and newness *per se* do not stand for greater humanity or interpersonal affection.

The Korean language reflects the resistance of shamanism to segmentation and dichotomization. Although it abounds in intricacies in interpersonal areas, the tenses of verbs are very simple. Nor are nouns, pronouns, or adjectives elaborated into an ornate system according to gender, number, or case. Until a few years ago, the Korean language lacked an equivalent for the English word "she." The first-person, singular, possessive pronoun is used with great reluctance; a monogamous wife is referred to as "our wife," in order to avoid the implication that the speaker wishes to withdraw his ego from the continuum of the community. In daily conversation, Koreans frequently omit the subject and object of a sentence—particularly when they are human beings. The speakers have such close rapport (ego continuum) that there is little failure of communication despite such incomplete sentences.

Death

To the shamanistic man, death is as much a part of existence as birth. Man continues to exist not only in the lives of his kindred—especially his offspring—but also in his own body. Death signifies neither the annihilation of human life, nor the commencement of nonhuman life in another world. For these reasons, the corpse of the shamanistic person is treated with affection and respect, and is attended to as if it retained all the senses with which to feel pain, cold, wet, hunger, and so forth. Beyond this, any shamanistic definition of death is simply too "fuzzy" to be of scientific use.

There is, for instance, no satisfactory answer to the question "what happens to the spirit or soul of the dead?" The only response which may approximate a logical answer is that, as one's vitality wanes and biological functions cease, life goes into a dormant state. As the corpse decomposes, the spirit decays with it. When the body has completely disappeared, the spirit also vanishes. Smooth and speedy decay is considered desirable, for it evinces the smooth flow of the rhythm of life. A burial site in which the normal course of decay is hindered is considered inauspicious. Disinterment is always a risky undertaking, liable to disturb the spirit of the dead. Elaborate *kut* are held to placate the spirit and to prevent any possible mishap from afflicting those who are responsible for the exhumation. The spirit may wander away from the buried body, but so long as the dead body remains comfortable and has no reason to seek vengeance among the living, the spirit normally remains with the body. In such a case, even if the spirit did wander away from the body, it would normally be harmless. On the other hand, if the dead person had intense ill-will at the time of his death, or if the body has been mistreated, the wandering spirit can wreak destruction on the living. Unless he can make amends with his spiritual tormentor, the victim of a vengeful spirit is helpless. Even if he is able to identify his tormentor through the help of a good *mudang*, the spirit is beyond further retaliation.

Just as in life, that which the corpse of a shamanistic man deplores most is loneliness. For this reason, elaborate rites of mourning, burial, and memorial are undertaken to reassure and maintain the warmth of kinship affection toward the dead. The continuing companionship, memory, and affection of the surviving family takes the sting out of death. The surviving child's affection diminishes loneliness and "warms" the cold grave. A person deprived of this companionship and affection is truly forsaken and wretched, and this is one of the primary reasons that every effort is made to secure a child; if there is no biological offspring, adoption is mandatory.

Despite the long history of Buddhism as the primary religion of Korea, cremation has rarely been practiced. The preferred practice of burial has always been a matter of solemn importance, and dwelling-places for the dead are considered of greater importance than those for the living. Under the influence of geomancy, originally developed in China, every plot of land has been thought to possess a "fortune" which affected the living conditions of those who inhabited it. This fortune is a kind of confluence of forces determined by geographical features. It is customary for Koreans to employ the service of a capable geomancer to locate a "fortunate" burial ground for the family. Innumerable folk tales have been told concerning the power, honor, longevity, wealth, and fertility which has come to those who have selected their burial places well.

Families that are endowed with financial resources usually manage to secure a "fortunate" burial ground in advance of its actual use. But if others should discover this ground, there is a risk that they may preempt the fortune contained therein by burying their relatives there. In such a case, the legal owner may threaten to exhume the corpse—thus prompting the thief to come forward and purchase the land legally—but the fortune is deemed to have been irreversibly appropriated by the first cadaverous occupant. In rural areas, the Korean courts are still asked to adjudicate disputes concerning geomantic rights to real estate. For judges whose legal training has been exclusively in European theories of property law, this type of litigation has been vexatious, to say the least. Since the relevant provisions of the civil code are almost exclusively Roman-Teutonic, the more conscientious judges have been compelled to teach themselves basic theories of geomancy. For the litigants, the entire problem is literally a matter of life and death.

Once the burial-place had been obtained, every effort was made to construct a posthumous residential environment which approximated as closely as possible the one in which the corpse had lived. For the rich and powerful, this meant constructing full-scale residences, complete with various chambers and a kitchen. For the less wealthy, the tomb was stocked with miniature replicas of the corpse's lifetime dwelling place. Both types of tombs were stocked with utensils, tableware, clothes, cosmetics, ornaments, foodstuffs, beverages, and so forth.

In ancient Korea, burial was delayed as long as possible for fear that unseemly haste would be interpreted as a sign of apathy or even antipathy. Even a death which occurred during the summer, or one resulting from a contagious disease, failed to hasten the burial. The finest hemp cloth was used to make a shroud, and a funeral procession brought the corpse to the tomb. Professional wailers were often employed, and the family expressed its sorrow in loud, intense, and frequent outpourings of emotion. Elegies were read or sung. For several months after the burial, regular meals were offered to the dead, and surviving kindred made every effort to visit the dead even after this period. Surviving sons were required to build a dwelling beside the tomb of their deceased parent and to keep him company around the clock for two years. A mourning son could travel only in sackcloth with a headgear which shielded his head from being seen. The son was considered a sinner for having failed to prolong the life of his parent, and he was expected to abstain from meat, wine, music, and sex during the mourning period. Conceiving a child during the mourning period was a supreme disgrace to the individual as well as to the entire lineage.

The rites of memorial on the anniversaries of the ancestral deaths have been commonly understood to be "ancestor worship." Although the visitors bow to the tomb on their arrival, on offering food, and on their departure, this is not considered worshipping in any religious sense. Just as the shamanistic man bows and offers food to his living parents, he does the same for them when they are dead; they are still his parents, and still are deserving of his respect and affection. Despite the insistent condemnations of the Christian churches, then, to the shamanistic man his rituals do not seem idolatrous.

II. Society and Social Life

The pervasive influence of shamanistic attitudes on Korean culture is frequently blamed for everything that is, and has been, "wrong" with Korea. Shamanistic revulsion toward harming others has chilled the martial fervor of the nation, and preoccupation with family matters has corrupted the nationalism and patriotism upon which modern Korea is based. In order to understand the impact of shamanism on Korean culture, then, it is necessary to consider the full range of beliefs and practices connected with it. The first part of this essay dealt with the aspects of Korean shamanism most closely connected with the individual, his life, and his family. In this part we will cast our net more widely and demonstrate the consequences of the shamanistic world-view on matters of social, political, and religious importance.

It should be noted at the outset that shamanistic values are not easily divided into strictly "private" and "public" spheres. Having rejected dualism in all other areas of life, it has been difficult for the shamanistic man to accept a dichotomy here, despite the historical reiteration of the Confucian elite that a distinction between the private and public was necessary. By contrast, it has always been easier for the shamanistic man to conceive of the country as a very large, extended family—with the ruler as its head—than to transfer his loyalty and affection to such abstractions as "nation," "state," or "commonwealth." Philosophically indisposed to distinguish between the public and private, the shamanistic man attempts to ensure that human affection and decency are maximized at the same time that social efficiency stability, and progress are facilitated. To accomplish this, the shamanistic world-view tries to adapt the overlapping continuum between the civic and the familial to serve the exigencies of a rapidly industrializing nation-state. In these efforts shamanism has so far experienced little success.

Ebb and Flow

To the shamanistic man, nothing is permanent. While he accepts the maxim "nothing good lasts forever," he insists that the opposite is also true, "nothing bad lasts forever." The forces of nature and life maintain a balance in human fortune; fortune sustained for a period of time signifies that the beginning of waning fortune is at hand. If one generation of a family enjoys too much wealth or good fortune it may use up the total wealth alloted for the family, creating a sort of overdraft which depletes the share belonging to future generations. The same is true in other areas of human endeavor; political power is rarely long-lived, perfection contains the seeds of deterioration, and extreme misery generates its own amelioration.

This view of life, which stresses the changing nature of human existence, tends to subdue the responses of Koreans regarding their emotional state. They hesitate to describe their lives as very good, and even in exchanging daily greetings the most optimistic response to the question "how are you?" is frequently a non-committal "so-so." This attitude has also affected the behavior of Koreans in other ways. Parents berate their children, for instance, out of fear that excessive love may bring ill luck to the child. The shamanistic man enjoys life modestly, through his personal relations with others, but he does not have faith in the "perfectibility" of man which might impel him to attempt to dominate his environment. He communes with nature and extolls its beauty and majesty in poetry and song. And he considers it part of the same existential continuum to which he belongs, rather than a group of features and forces which must be overcome in order to provide man with a suitable environment. This is in direct contrast to the activities of Western science, the goal of which is to abolish the need for man to adapt to nature by creating increasingly artificial, controlled environments. The lack of any ideal of permanence has precluded Korean shamanism from accepting the idea that man is "perfectible," or that he can attain the absolute enjoyment of natural rights to life, liberty, and property. To the shamanistic man, all these are subject to the ebb and flow which are part of life and nature.

Just as the shamanistic man lacks any ideal of permanence, he lacks also any ideals which can be described as "absolute convictions." Since he lacks an absolute god to define ethical standards, the shamanistic man has no simple black-and-white dualism against which to judge the goodness, justice, or righteousness of his actions. Instead, he is condemned to persistent self-doubt, and becomes hopelessly mired in a complicated calculus of interpersonal dynamics. Since the shamanistic man has never considered wealth, longevity, political power, or honor to be consequences of divine blessing, he has never been able to persuade himself that militant and deadly measures to defend them are justifiable. The fact that, in other cultures, theft of property is punishable by death is simply appalling to the shamanistic man. This attitude has given rise to some interesting conflicts. When a rapid influx of the rural population into urban areas resulted in a proliferation of "squatters" on privately owned property, for instance, the owners of the land found themselves poweless to expel the intruders. Legal provisions were useless, since the property owners could not gain public support in favor of forcible eviction, and eventually extralegal means were found to remove the squatters from the land. The owners finally agreed to compensate the squatters if they would leave. The basic human rights of the propertyless were, in this instance, given priority over the legal rights of the property owners.

Civil Conflict

In Judeo-Christian cultures civil conflicts are usually resolved through adjudication, the formal and public process through which the right and wrong of the parties in dispute is determined. Just as the supreme and absolute deity in these cultures is the law-giver, so also is he the ultimate judge and final arbiter of human affairs. Law, in these cultures, tends to be abstract, and justice, a mutually exclusive judgment of right and wrong. Adjudication settles disputes by authoritatively designating one party to be wholly in the right, and the other wholly in the wrong, neither party can be partially right or wrong. In these cultures the dominant inclination is to bring civil conflicts into public view, and to judge according to abstract legal rules which are designed to create objectivity and to minimize the influence of particular equities or of emotion.

By contrast, the shamanistic man prefers to settle civil conflicts through non-adjudicatory means. For him, the procedure of officializing and publicizing a conflict only intensifies the ill will of the parties involved. When the conflict becomes a matter of public record, members of the community are drawn into the conflict by their testimony, siding with one or the other of the parties. This serves only to increase the antagonism and maximize the distance between the partisans. Moreover, even if adjudication results in a decision which is both fair and just, it rarely resolves the emotional conflict between the parties. This continuing animosity disrupts the rhythm of communal life, and makes it impossible to restore communal solidarity. Having been publicly declared wrong, the loser of an adjudicated dispute is unable to restore normal relations with either his opponent or with the remainder of the community. All of this is deeply disturbing to the shamanistic man.

The shamanistic preference for resolving civil conflicts is conciliation, in which the goal is to achieve an amicable and agreeable settlement. Deciding which side is right, and which wrong, is not the primary interest, nor is there any attempt to publicize the proceedings or to follow the guidelines of an abstract set of legal rules. A settlement which maximizes the emotional satisfaction of each party and minimizes the post-settlement resentment is the fair resolution. Conciliation avoids the items which disturb the shamanistic man about adjudication. Since there is no public record, the parties in the dispute are more easily reconciled after a settlement has been reached, and members of the community need not make public their views on the matter. The privacy of the conciliation process prevents a further escalation of mutual antipathy, and avoids disrupting the rhythm of communal life.

The privacy of the conciliation process, however, is really only a fiction, for while it is going on the parties in conflict undergo subtle but intense pressure to achieve a settlement. The entire community lets its preferred mode of settlement be known to the parties in dispute, with the implicit threat that if such a settlement is not brought about the parties will be ostracized. This type of pressure is most difficult to ignore. The community has a legitimate interest in any conflict which may arise among its members because of its propensity to disrupt the life of the community. In shamanistic society, the community does not hesitate to use its influence to minimize these disruptions.

Denial of Conflict

Whenever possible, the shamanistic man desires to avoid even the process of conciliation by achieving a consensus that no civil conflict ever existed. Instead, he will say that there was a misunderstanding which was wrongly perceived to be a conflict and the abundant humanity of the concerned parties had only to exert itself to correct the dangerous misperception. This type of resolution strengthens communal solidarity, and may even increase interpersonal affection.

This predisposition to "deny conflict to the death" contrasts sharply with the practices in other cultures, which would view the shamanistic practice as ineffectual escapism. In Western culture, conflict can never be resolved unless it is accepted as real and subjected to a full and open debate. Without such a reasoned discussion the conflict would fester, and would create an even larger problem to be solved later on. But the shamanistic reluctance to acknowledge the existence of conflict is not merely procrastination; it stems, rather, from the concern that public conflicts may become more difficult to resolve because of the adversary relationship they force upon the parties involved. The shamanistic man desires to keep the relationship between the parties within the realm of neighborliness, and to resolve conflicts through mutual concession and compromise.

The underlying premise of the shamanistic view is that no one, not even the victim of a crime, can be either absolutely right or absolutely wrong. Extenuating circumstances may explain the actions of a robber, and the victim may have been wrong to make himself such a tempting target. Conflict is resolved through the rejection of the absolute and abstract.

In civil disputes the stress on mutual concession and compromise is incomparably greater. From earliest childhood, every "decent" member of shamanistic society is trained to avoid any course of action which might lead to confrontation with another. A well-bred person is one whose sensitivity is so refined that he may detect far in advance the possibility of conflict, and who promptly modifies his behavior in order to minimize the conflict. The greater the delicacy and alertness with which a person carries out this operation, the greater is his virtue. This refined sensibility, *nunch'i* (eye sensitivity), is the quintessence of shamanistic cultural refinement. A person who lacks this sensitivity is an alien, while one whose sense is underdeveloped is considered vulgar, if not barbarous.

Although readiness to modify one's behavior carries no overt requirement that others reciprocate, reciprocation is expected of cultivated persons. If a person lacks sufficient cultivation to reciprocate in such situations, others gradually exclude him from the regular orbit of communal interaction. The rest of the community no longer feels constrained to exercise *nunch'i* with regard to such a rude person. Thus, even though no balance sheet is kept, the communal memory maintains a meticulous account: reciprocity is of the essence if a shamanistic man is to keep up his relations with the community.

Since concessions frequently take place unobtrusively and far in advance of any actual conflict, an "uncivilized" or foreign person may be unaware that some reciprocation is required of him. If the outsider persists in his "shameless pushiness," the accumulated exasperation of the community often explodes into open hostility. The outsider, unprepared for such a sudden and unprovoked outburst of resentment, might easily take offense at what he considers "Korean uncivility." Participation in the communal interactions of shamanistic culture has always been a risky proposition for an outsider, particularly because the values which guide these interactions are amorphous and unarticulated even among those who belong to the community. In a cross-cultural setting, then, the very rules which shamanistic culture has developed to avoid conflict may become the cause of conflict.

Criminal Justice

The shamanistic sense of penal justice has not been concerned with treating convicted criminals humanely, because the guilty are automatically considered to be expelled from the human race for their crimes. But shamanism has been concerned with preventing criminals from being formally and publicly declared guilty, so that, whatever else the criminal might suffer, at least he might retain his humanity. As a result, there has been a strong disinclination toward governmental prosecution of non-capital offenses because the consequences were so harsh, inflexible, and irreversible. Even a private flogging, though susceptible to abuse, was a better alternative because it allowed the criminal to retain his membership in the community.

The most suitable solution for the criminal in shamanistic society is to confess. By doing so he redeems his humanity, retains his membership in the community, and agrees to accept the punishment for his deeds. For the shamanistic community, the advantages of confession were that it moderated the desire of the victims for revenge, it lessened the amount by which the humanity of the community was diminished by allowing the criminal to retain his membership, and it allowed the community to escape from the pain a trial would inevitably bring. Confession vindicated the justice of the communal norms and avoided making an unwilling victim of a convicted criminal.

Capital punishment poses a difficulty for shamanistic culture. However justified, the destruction of human life has been considered abhorrent. A condemned pregnant woman, for instance, was normally given a reprieve until her child was old enough to be viable. Executions were never carried out in spring—the season of life's renewal—but were postponed until autumn. Moreover, no regular member of the community dared serve as executioner; for this task Koreans employed foreigners who lived outside the community and were not considered part of it. These foreigners married only among themselves, and resisted any attempt by shamanistic communities to assimilate them. The general populace held these foreigners in awe because of the apparent immunity with which they shed human blood; even the powerful curses of their victims seemed to have no effect upon them.

Shamanism and Politics

Although the shamanistic world-view places great emphasis on providing an ethical framework for members of the community, the shamanistic man has always found the "logic" of power extremely intractable. In large measure this is due to the inherent dualism of political power. In traditional Korean society there was no middle ground between loyalty and treachery, and the Confucian elite which held political power did little to moderate the harsh edges of this distinction. As with all sorts of dualistic thought, the Confucian approach to political power has always made the shamanistic man quite uneasy.

Confucian political theory drew a clear distinction—quite foreign to shamanistic thought—between the interpersonal relations dominant in the community and the political processes connected with the holding of power. Although the Confucian elite acknowledged that politics was dehumanizing, it nevertheless excused the failings of the system because the ways of power were considered "extraordinary." To be sure, the Confucian elite attempted to humanize politics as much as possible by insisting that those who held power be abundantly humane. Moderating influences were also exercised by the pluralistic input of the *I Ching* (Book of Change) and by classic Taoism. Without these, the pernicious effect of Confucian dualism might have been greater than it was. But despite all attempts to humanize the political process, those who wished to mitigate the harshness of power dynamics were no match for those who adroitly exploited the dualistic fabric of politics. Inevitably, politics came to be monopolized by specialists who refused to be rendered impotent in the name of humanization. It is no wonder that, in the face of the Confucian failure to humanize politics, shamanistic man made every attempt to flee from the arena of political power.

Because he perceives power politics to be indecent and vile, and because they seem to impose adversary relationships and confrontations, the shamanistic man has avoided politics whenever possible. Korean shamanism has never attempted to formulate an effective alternative to the Confucian theory of politics, but has instead sought to disassociate itself from the arena of power. Naturally, it has not always been possible for shamanism to remain unaffected by those in power. But while a given ruler might be feared by shamanistic society, he was not necessarily respected, and shamanistic communities did not hesitate to rebel against rulers who were vicious or did not adequately provide for the people under their care. The opposition of shamanistic society, however, was limited to driving out individuals who had shown themselves to be wicked; there was never any attempt to oppose the Confucian system itself.

Conformity

One of the major reasons that shamanism has failed to provide an alternative to Confucian political theory is the great value which shamanism attaches to conformity—itself a logical corollary of the shamanistic fear of personal isolation and loneliness. Individuality, regardless of how it is expressed, suggests a desire to separate oneself from others; it creates a boundary between the individual and the community which the shamanistic man fears and abhors. In the interest of conformity, then, shamanistic man avoids many types of behavior. This is particularly true in politics, where the shamanistic man is generally reluctant to contradict or disagree publicly with others. Since shamanistic ethics are designed to prevent or eliminate disagreements and conflicts, rather than to humanize or civilize them, they have never developed rules of "civilized public disagreement." Indeed, to the shamanistic man, the very idea of "civilized conflict" is absurd. Unlike Western culture, Korean shamanism does not admit that "gentlemanly rules and regulations" (which, in the West, govern everything from boxing to warfare) are able to transform the quality of the conflict. To the shamanistic mind, "regulated warfare" is still warfare, and it should be prevented.

The shamanistic desire for conformity hungers, in turn, for authoritative guidance, and stimulates authoritarianism in the exercise of political power. Guided by a strong authority, conformity can bring about stability and order; without authority, conformity breeds confusion and chaos. Because of its refusal to create public disagreement, the shamanistic impulse toward conformity is easily seized upon by radical extremists or any other strong authority. By sheer force of personality, a strong and charismatic leader can easily sway a conforming public for some time; but that same public may just as easily be swayed to the opposite extreme by another leader.

Loyalty

The propensity of shamanistic conformists to flit from one

extreme to the other, creating a condition of chronic instability, has been exacerbated by the importation of democracy into Korea. This is because the anti-authoritarian individualism and institutionalized adversary relations of democracy run directly counter to the traditional shamanistic sense of loyalty. Korean politicians are familiar and at ease with the concept of personal loyalty; but in the view of shamanism, personal loyalty has value because it is unselfish and perpetual. The idea that loyalty can be dissolved after a term of years or subjected to self-serving impulses— as is commonly the case in democratic politics—strikes the shamanistic man as very strange.

To the shamanistic man, the deliberate maintenance of institutionalized adversary relations is an even stranger feature of democracy than its attitude toward personal loyalty. The dialectical tension maintained by the two-party system is repugnant because it requires a man to carry on a perpetual and public opposition which is both emotionally and culturally painful. Also, the idea of a "loyal opposition" strikes the shamanistic man as contradictory, since lasting opposition is anything but a sign of loyalty. The shamanistic mind is emotionally unable to embrace the need for perpetual opposition between those who are in power and those who are not. If conflicts exist, shamanistic ethics require that compromise and conciliation be exercised in order to bring about a settlement; even regulated opposition cannot long survive if shamanistic ethics are brought into play.

Shamanism and Democracy

Modern Korea, with its foundations in shamanistic views that do not mesh easily with the imported patterns of democracy, has experienced a great deal of frustration and disappointemnt in dealing with democratic politics. As a result, national self-criticism has lamented the innately "undemocratic" strain in the national character, while at the same time denigrating democracy as inherently un-Korean, unrealistic, unsuitable, and inefficient. Although there is some truth to this, the real problem stems from the fact that the cultural background of Korea has not yet adjusted to the new rules that govern the exercise of political power. Without a fully internalized sense of democracy and its requirements, the Korean experiment has foundered. Political funding has led to unbridled corruption, bipartisan agreement has come to imply that a "dirty sellout" has taken place, and the way toward true compromise has been blocked by the stigma of betrayal of principle which is hurled at the compromisors. Even the comparative integrity of personal loyalty has been unable to mitigate the difficulties of democratic policies in Korea, since the democratic idea of loyalty is itself foreign to the Korean way of thinking. In Western democracy, for instance, extensive personal loyalty (of the sort practiced by the shamanistic man) carries with it the risk of nepotism, sectionalism, authoritarianism, and the cult of personality. But to the Korean mind, personal loyalty to the head of a political party deserves its reward, and the assignment of political offices is still made on this basis.

Despite the strong desire of the Republic of Korea to emulate the West in all areas of national life, the remnants of indigenous culture have continued to be accorded a somewhat bashful legitimacy. Even among those who are firmly convinced that the adoption of an American-style democracy is not only right and proper but somehow inevitable, the desire to maintain cultural continuity with the past by retaining that which is "useful and beneficial" has found strong support. The interaction of indigenous shamanism and imported democracy, however, has not always made for an easy coexistence.

The high expectations which Koreans have come to associate with Western democracy have made it even more difficult to maintain contact with indigenous culture. American-style democracy has come to be viewed as a respectable and coveted symbol that confirms Korea's status as an advanced and developed nation. There has also been a widespread expectation that an American-style democracy would bring about an American standard of living, with all the wealth, power, and industrial advancement that it has come to represent. Just as the elite of ancient Korea believed that faithful observance of Confucian orthodoxy would produce perennial good harvests, peace, and tranquility, the intellectuals of modern Korea treat democracy as an orthodoxy which will bring tangible benefits in its wake. Even

Christianity has benefitted from the Korean desire for democracy, since, in the Korean mind, Christianity is identified with American-style democracy. In the view of many modern Koreans, then, the rejection of indigenous culture in favor of democracy and Christianity is imperative if Korea is to reap the bounty of membership in the modern world.

Nevertheless, the manner in which democracy has so far been practiced in Korea has been afflicted with an air of unreality. The limitation of governmental power, for instance, is unrealistic in Korea because it precludes the creation of a strong and effective government to carry out the modernization of the nation. And yet, it is the limitation of governmental absolutism which is one of the major thrusts of democracy. The civilian control of all aspects of govern-ment—also a basic tenet of American-style democracy—fails to take into account the serious external military threat under which the Republic of Korea has labored; in this sense also, Korean democracy has been unrealistic.

Even more than the confusing theoretical bases of democracy, the everyday practices of democratic politicians have perplexed the Korean people. Political funding, for instance, strikes the modern Korean as a particularly corrupt aspect of democracy. Since the primary goal of a political party is to get and keep political power, the notion of a political contribution made merely out of patriotism or a sense of civic duty, without any expectation of tangible favor in return, scarcely sounds convincing. The same suspicion of bribery extends to elections. Votes are frequently cast on the basis of what tangible advantages a candidate is expected to produce for the voter. Every vote seems to be bought, if not with cash or merchandise, at least with promises of political favors. To the Korean voter, democracy has only introduced more convuluted formalities; it has not halted the sale of political offices and favors.

Traditionally, the surest sign of shamelessness has been to brag about oneself or one's relatives. But electoral campaigns are an institutionalized public competition in self-glorification. No candidate could possibly win an election through modesty and self-deprecation, yet these are precisely the virtues which shamanistic culture has accustomed Koreans to expect of "decent" human beings. Equally important, political candidates must denigrate their opponents—a sort of depravity which Koreans consider less than human, especially when it is motivated by greed and a desire to enhance one's own self-conceit.

The debasement of humanity which seems to accompany democracy has caused the Korean people to hold professional politicians in low esteem. High echelon bureaucrats, by comparison, are more respected; at least they obtained their positions through the scrupulously fair civil service examinations rather than through the demeaning and venal political process. It is the sad misfortune of the Korean nation that the traditional cultural values of humanity and decency seem incompatible with electoral democracy, while actions traditionally regarded as shameless and depraved seem indispensable civic virtues.

Shamanism and Communism

Although the relatively recent division of the Korean peninsula into two independent nations has disrupted the historical and cultural unity of the region, it has not been able to erase the traditional biases of Korean culture. The communist regime of North Korea—no less than the Republic of Korea in the south—has had to come to terms with shamanism. On the surface, it would seem that the anti-humanitarian attitudes of communism, and its disregard of human life in the name of revolutionary struggle, would leave little common ground between shamanism and communism. At the same time, however, the paternalistic egalitarianism and collectivist bias of communism have been offered an amenable reception by the indigenous political culture.

Just as interesting is the tenacious grip which the personality-cult of Kim Ilsung and his family has managed to gain on the communist ruling circle. Despite the efforts of the North Koreans to destroy traditional familialism—the archenemy of the socialist "construction"—Kim has been officially declared the "parent of the nation", and popular adulation is directed toward his entire family. Kim has been made out to be an extraordinarily capable shaman, in a genuinely traditional sense; the fecundity of hens and the fertility of fruit trees have both been attributed to the actions of the "Great and Beloved Leader." When one recalls that the primary function and essential qualification for a shaman was to ensure productivity and fertility in every aspect of human endeavor, this aspect of Kim's personality-cult is quite suggestive.

Naturally, all the sensitive and important positions in the communist party and government are being monopolized by Kim's relatives, but it is the adulation of Kim's dead forebears that is truly remarkable. The politicized biographies of Kim's mother, father, uncles, grandfather, and so on, would make the most fervent biographers of the founder of the Chosŏn dynasty green with envy. It would appear that Kim's rule is being transformed into a hereditary monarchy, and if this is so, one is forced to believe that shamanism has gained the upper hand in its interactions with imported Marxist-Leninism.

Religious Tolerance

Although Northeast Asia has not traditionally adhered to a strict separation of church and state, such as is common in Western democracies, Korean shamanism has never successfully competed with other religions for political power and influence. Part of the reason for this is that shamanism has never elaborated itself ecclesiastically or doctrinally, thus allowing the better-organized religions, Buddhism and Confucianism, to obtain recognition as the orthodoxy of the ruling elite. It is also true, however, that "moral imperialism" has never been a characteristic of Korean shamanism, which suggests that it never seriously attempted to compete with other religions.

Instead of overt opposition to the encroachments of imported religions, shamanism offered only its inherent resiliency and tolerance. If imported religions were to become acceptable to Koreans, they soon found it necessary to "shamanize" themselves. In this way, much of the shamanistic world-view has influenced Korean culture out of all proportion to the political import of shamanism. The merging process also operated in the other direction; the shamanistic man feels no qualms about showing reverence or paying tribute to all the deities established by various religions. Many Chinese heroes, Buddha and bodhisattvas, and Korean folk heroes have often found their way into the chants of a *mudang*. By worshipping many deities, the shamanistic man hopes to improve his chances that the aid of one will prove efficacious; if more than one responds, so much the better.

Because of the basic similarities between the Confucian and shamanistic world-views, the relations between them have always been close. Like shamanism, Confucianism stressed the importance of family, kinship, loyalty, old age, and respect for the environment, and it had an antipathy toward militarism. In view of these shared values, shamanisn was able to overcome its resistance to the pedantic, extremely patrilinear, hierarchical inequality which it found in Confucianism. There can be little doubt that the strength of Confucianism in Korean social and cultural life owes much to its basic congruity with indigenous Korean shamanism.

Although shamanism also found some elements of Buddhism agreeable (such as its aversion to the destruction of animal life, its apolitical orientation, and its belief in the inexorability of reward and retribution), more serious disagreements obstructed close relations between the two. The most important of these were the Buddhist obsession with the metaphysical and transcendent, and its insistence that enlightenment could be secured only on an individual basis through one's own efforts. To the shamanistic mind it was imperative that enlightenment be attainable on a family basis, so that any member of a family might secure it for all his relatives. No decent shamanistic individual would think of attaining enlightenment if it meant that he would have to leave his relatives and enjoy it selfishly. Before it was accepted by the Korean people, then, Buddhism had to dilute its individualism and become more familial in its doctrine.

In its interactions with Buddhism and Confucianism, Korean shamanism reinforced those beliefs and practices which were congenial to its own values. More fundamentally, the fact that neither of these religions were monotheistic or absolutist rendered their world-views basically compatible with shamanism. Although the shamanistic man is capable of accepting an absolute, monotheistic god who demands exclusive loyalty, there is a limit to his adherence to such a god: he would retain his faith only so long as the god proved to be effectual in tangible ways.

In the long run, merely abstract and intellectual experiences are insufficient for the shamanistic man. Instead, he desires sensory experience—preferably of a sort amenable to communal sharing—as proof of a god's existence. Christian churchmen, for instance, have observed rather ruefully that Korean Christians tend to importune god for worldly benefits rather than to praise him or to pray for eternal salvation. Another tenet of Christianity, as espoused by the missionaries who spread the gospel to Korea, has been illustrated by a conversation between an American Protestant missionary and a Korean. The missionary explained his gospel and urged the Korean to become a Christian in order to avoid the horrible damnation awaiting the heathens in hell, and instead, to go to heaven for the eternal bliss in store for the Christians. The Korean responded by asking the missionary where his dead parents were, in heaven or in hell. Since they had died without becoming Christians, the missionary said, they could not have gone to heaven. As with enlightenment in Buddhism, the Korean responded that a son's place is with his parents, be it heaven or hell, and that it would be the height of depravity for him to separate himself from all his forbears by attaining an individual salvation. The refusal of Christianity to make any doctrinal modifications for the sake of its Korean flock has no doubt contributed to the difficulties which Koreans have had in accepting the religion.

Modern Challenges

Few Koreans believe that the shamanistic world-view is adequate or appropriate for the challenges of the modern world. Even among those conservatives who wish to maintain the shamanistic heritage, the tolerance and malleability which characterize shamanism seem to be far from laudable traits, since they facilitate their own disintegration. The view of modern reformers, those who would drag Korea into

Western modernization at any cost, is even less charitable. To them, shamanism is a disgrace which is better forgotten. Most educated Koreans are embarrassed if shamanism becomes a topic of conversation, especially in the presence of a foreigner. They are quick to deny that shamanism has had anything to do with "decent folks," and even quicker to terminate the discussion by proclaiming that shamanism is no longer a part of Korean life. The general aversion to shamanism among contemporary Koreans is so strong that few entertainers would admit that they had relatives who were *mudangs*.

In this critical context, shamanism has received the blame for many of the ills of modern Korea. The lack of a shamanistic desire for military conquest has been accused of contributing to the status of Korea as a small and weak nation. Shamanistic respect for the aged has been viewed as cultural "backwardness," which has prevented Korea from attaining modernization. And the lack of a questing, domineering spirit in shamanism has been blamed for the failure of Koreans to develop their skills in science and technology.

The avarice of many *mudangs* has further aggravated the misfortunes of shamanism. Rather than providing competent service which would reinforce communal solidarity, reaffirm the joy of life, and promote the healing of psychogenic and psychosomatic illness, some *mudangs* intimidate people with their supposed superhuman powers for the purpose of exacting money. By luring people with promises of good fortune, many *mudangs* encouraged dissipation and idleness.

Clearly, the modern challenges to shamanism are serious threats to its continued existence. Already, modernization, Westernization, urbanization, industrialization, the development of science and technology (and especially of mass communication), the vigorous propagation of Christianity, the humiliation of colonial servitude under Japan, and the continuing struggle against North Korea,have all exacted a heavy toll. As the breakdown of familialism and increase of individualism continue, shamanism is sure to be affected even further. There is some question whether the shamanistic world-view can survive without the social structures that have traditionally provided its bases.

It is too early to sound the death-knell for Korean shamanism, however, and Korea's experiment with modernization has been fortunate to have had such a tolerant and adaptable world-view. A more militant and absolutist religious tradition might have slowed the pace of change even further, and would certainly have made change more painful. A good illustration is provided by the remarkable success of family planning in Korea during the past two decades. Anyone who had been at all familiar with the traditional craving of Koreans for children would have given the birth control program a very slim chance of success. But it did succeed, by stressing the practical and palpable benefits of smaller families to those who had already been born. The problem of abortion has caused little political strife in Korea (except among Korean Christians), since the shamanistic consensus is that the parental decision in this regard is beyond public interference.

The Future

Despite frustrations and disappointments, the people of Korea are committed to democracy as their national future. Even with all the cross-cultural dissonance, they seem to believe there is no better system in practice. But before they can begin to enjoy the fruits of liberal democracy, a cultural revolution must occur which will destroy the shamanistic world-view and replace it with the views of modern democracy. This is a gargantuan enterprise in cultural engineering, for which there is no successful precedent, but it may be that in Korea the development of industrial capitalism will prove to be a truly effective agent for cultural revolution.

Already the shamanistic world-view shows serious signs of erosion due to the influences of industrial capitalism: familialism is declining, individualism is increasing, youth and innovation have begun to displace age and tradition, and quantitative measures have begun to replace the qualitative as indicators of value. In short, the perspectives and practices of the industrial middle class are slowly being introduced into the Korean world-view.

It seems likely that until the new, bourgeois values have been fully internalized by the Korean people there will be some confusion and disorder. Freed from the constraints of personal loyalty and familialism which have hitherto constrianed it, political power may be used in brutal and totalitarian ways until the democratic system of checks and balances is finally assimilated by the Koreans. It is impossible to predict the future of Korean shamanism and its world-view in light of the many changes through which Korean society is presently passing. But the path which Korea has chosen is overtly political and, given its apolitical character, shamanism may prove to be no match for other, more militant world-views.

Korean Taoism and Shamanism

A side from a book entitled *Korean Taoism* by Nŭng-Yi Lee, which is both a systematic study and a collection of source materials relating to Taoism in Korea, the subject has been generally ignored. There have been some specialized studies in the field of philosophical and religious studies,[1] but the topic has been largely overlooked in studies of, or introductions to, Korean religions.[2] Yet without a discussion of Korean Taoism, the study of Korean religion as a whole would be incomplete. Korean Taoism exists not only as an historical fact but as a present day reality and is an essential component of Korean religion and culture. Many sources for the study of Korean Taoism can be found in traditional materials,[3] and the present paper draws upon them. However, this study does not include an investigation of the Chinese background of Taoism.

This study is intended as a contribution to an understanding of the background of Korean religions, and especially of the new religions: it will also be useful in any examination of the origins and development of Taoism outside of China, and will also be of help in discovering the origins of Japanese Taoism.[4]

The origin of Korean Taoism is lost in antiquity, even though the Korean Taoist text *Kyuwŏn sahwa,* suggests that the ancient Korean Shamanistic ideal of the Tan'gun myth was an influence in Chinese Taoism.[5]

However,, Tan'gun (24th century B.C. by traditional Korean reckoning)[6] is also believed by some scholars to be related to *"tan'gul,"* an ancient Korean word that had the same meaning as the Mongolian word *tengri,* which means shaman.[7] The word is also interpreted by using the Chinese characters for *tan* and *gun* to mean "birth tree" and "the lord" respectively. The term *Lord* (Korean *kun,* Chinese *chun*) is also used of Taoist deities such as Hwang-Lao-Chun and Ti-Chun. The three deities of Taoism correspond to the trinity in the Tan'gun myth;—Hwan-in, Hwan-ung, Tan'gun.

Tan'gun is also believed to have lived to the age of 1,908 and then to have become a mountain god, a fact which seems to be related to the ideal of immortality, an aspect of Taoism.

These arguments and the Taoist aspect of the Tan'gun myth are very interesting; and the idea that Taoist elements seem traceable in ancient Korea certainly deserve to be further examined, but this study is more concerned with investigating the arrival of Chinese Taoism into Korea, reviewing its historical development, indicating the characteristics of Korean Taoism and its relationship with shamanism, and finally, discussing the characteristics of Taoism in modern Korean culture.

I. An Historical Review of Korean Taoism and Its Characteristics

Emperor Ch'in Shih-huang-ti of the Ch'in dynasty is said to have sent Han Chung and the Taoist priest, Hsu Shih to bring back the elixir of life from the so-called "three sacred mountains".[8] This was probably a reference to Korea and the mountains referred to could, in fact, be Taebaek-san. Han Chung may also have been the person, Mahan, who became king of one of the Han states in Korea. Both names are based on the same Chinese character, which lends credence to an idea derived from Chinese sources,[9] but it is very difficult to prove that the place actually was Korea, even though there is both possibility and probability in the argument.

According to the *Samguk sagi (History of the Three Kingdoms)* Taoism was introduced into Koguryŏ in the year 624 A.D. In that year King Yŏngryu sent an envoy to T'ang China requesting some Taoist calendars, books, pictures and other items depicting respect for the deities. He also requested that some Taoist priests be sent who would help in spreading this new religion. In response, T'ang Kao-tsu and T'ai-tsung (618-649) both sent Taoist priests with images of the Heavenly Emperor, and they also lectured on Taoist teachings.[10] Even though it is generally believed that the beginning of Taoism in Koguryŏ was in 624 A.D., as indicated above, it seems clear from an investigation of the facts, that Taoism came to Koguryŏ much earlier than this date.

If Wang In and Ajiki brought Taoism to Japan in 602 A.D. from Paekche,[11] then Taoism existed in Paekche long before that date, and since Koguryŏ was geographically closer to mainland China than Paekche, it seems difficult to believe that Taoism came to Koguryŏ some twenty years later than to Japan.

There is a good deal of other evidence. First, due to the aftermath of wars in their own country during the fourth and third centuries B.C., many Chinese, especially those on the losing side, arrived in Korea bringing with them their beliefs, among them both Confucianism and Taoism. Educated Chinese often gave loyalty to both belief systems.[12]

Secondly, ancient Korea was frequently invaded by the Chinese as, for example, by the state known as Yen in China. The Chinese general Wi-man (194 B.C.?) even sought to build his own state in Korea.[13] Furthermore, China set up a colony consisting of three Commanderies on the peninsula in Han times and may have brought not only Chinese classics—both Confucian and Taoist—to Korea but also Taoist practices as well.

Thirdly, during the later Han dynasty when a warlord from eastern China invaded Koguryŏ (about 29 A.D.), Tae Mu-shin and the Koguryŏ army used tactics of strategic retreat to draw the invaders into their territory, then attacked and repulsed the enemy.[14] This method of passive defense seems to have been a direct result of Taoist influence, though Koguryŏ may also have known of the teachings of Sun Tzu.

Fourthly, tombs dating from the 2nd century A.D. in Korea bear such evidence of Chinese influence as the Taoistic images of immortals, the four mystical animals,etc., and this is also true of other tombs built in the 4th and 5th centuries, A.D.[15]

From these various bits of evidence it seems clear that Taoism existed in Koguryŏ long before its "official" entry in the year 624 A.D.

Taoism in the Three Kingdoms

A. Koguryŏ: One of the most important characteristics of Koguryŏ Taoism is that it seems early to have been accepted as something akin to an "official religion", which did not happen in any other period of

Koguryŏ history, nor indeed in the history of Japan.

In 642 A.D., King Pojang changed the policy of official patronage in favour of a more even-handed treatment of Taoism, Buddhism and Confucianism.

The high minister, Yŏn'gae-somun protested, saying,

> "Confucianism and Buddhism are popular among the people, but there are only a few believers in the mysterious doctrines of Lao Tzu, even though the yellow-capped preachers teach Taoism, telling the people that if they worship Lao Tzu they can become *sinsŏn* (Taoist Immortals) and ascend to heaven like the founder of the religion whose name was Togyo, or Song-go. We should therefore dispatch another envoy to China to invite more missionaries." [16]

In his view, Taoism seemed to be not only superior to Buddhism and Confucianism but also to the native religions of Koguryŏ. Because of this, Podok-hwang, a famous Koguryŏ Buddhist monk, expostulated with the king and sought not to have Taoism spread in competition with Buddhism. The king, however, did not believe that competition would divide the nation and consequently refused to accept the monk's appeal. The monk then left for Packche. [17]

Yŏn'gae-somun's strong support of Taoism made it the first official religion of Koguryŏ though one of his motives was certainly to cement good relations with China, where Taoism was strongly supported by the T'ang dynasty. The T'ang imperial family, whose surname was Li, in fact claimed direct descent from the founder of Taoism, Lao Tzu, who shared their surname. [18]

A second reason for his support was that he seemed to want to weaken Buddhist power which was aligned with his political opponents and to strengthen his own political power with Taoist support. [19]

Koguryŏ Taoism was basically Shamanistic Taoism. It seems to have consisted of the *Wu tou mi chiao* [20] or the cult of the Five Pecks of Rice of Chang Hsing (?-17 in which exorcism and the use of amulets was prominent. [21] *Wu tou mi chiao* also involved shamanistic practices, so that for instance, each year on the third day of the third lunar month

its followers worshipped Heaven and a sacred mountain as shamanistic gods, though with some Taoist overtones.[22] This led to the
building of Taoist temples and a consequent increase in the popularity
of Taoism; so much so that for a time it overshadowed Buddhism and
Confucianism.[23] Some scholars suggest that Taoism appealed to the
Koguryŏ temperament and was easily adapted to and synthesized with
the indigenous shamanism.[24]

According to the foundation myth of Koguryŏ,[25] a heavenly god
united both with an earthly woman, and with Tongmyŏng (the
founder of Koguryŏ), an idea which seems to be modeled on the Taoist
Trinity, or three gods idea.

Also, Haemuru came from heaven, and after giving birth to Yu
hwa returned to heaven.[26] This is very similar to the Taoist idea of the
"true heavenly man" who is said to have descended from heaven in a
dragon chariot and then returned.[27] Other mythological figures like
Hae mo su and Hwang ji are also said to have ascended to heaven.[28]

There is also the evidence from the Koruryŏ tombs which show a
Taoist and shamanistic synthesis, for example, depictions of: a fairy,
the dipper, the four mystical animals, the old man, medicine grasses,
and certain art forms.[29]

Koguryŏ Taoism was a religion of "defense of the land", Yŏn'gae-
somun seems to have been the most prominent advocate of Taoism in
Korea, and his plan was that Koguryŏ should imitate the T'ang model
and build a strong nation. The palace in the capital city had originally
been shaped like a half-moon but under the influence of Taoist
teaching, it was renovated to resemble a full moon, which was
regarded as more lucky for the nation.[30] As we have seen, Tae Musin's
army used the methods of Taoist passivity to defend Koguryŏ, and
other sources tell of hermits clothed in white, and Taoist soldiers, who
practiced the techniques of long-life and the martial arts for the
defense of the nation.[31]

B. Packche: The *Chou shu,* one of the Chinese dynastic histories,
records "there are many Buddhist monks and nuns and temples and
pagodas, but there are no Taoist priests (in Packche).[32] If the report is
accurate, it seems there was little interest in Taoism in the state of

Paekche. According to the *Annals of Paekche* in the *Samguk sagi*, however, Taoism was not unknown in Paekche. One passage says that after King Kŭn'gusu had destroyed the Koguryŏ army and was in pursuit of the enemy, his general, Mukohae, advised him that the enemy was thoroughly defeated and that further harassment was not necessary. Mukohae gently reinforced his suggestion with a quotation from the Taoist text, *Tao te Ching 44:*

> He who is contented suffers no disgrace
> He who knows when to stop is far from danger.[33]

Another section of the same work quotes the *Chuang Tzu:* "If you know your mistake, you are not to correct it. If you listen to one's expostulation, this is more extreme, and could even be called rude, (or violent temper)."[34]

Also, a shaman is said to have told King Uija: "Packche is like the moon, which means "full" (complete). If it is full it will decline, and if it is like the new moon, this means it is not yet full. Therefore if it is not yet full it will become gradually full."[35] This notion is prominent in Taoist thought.

A statue of an infant found in the tomb of King Muyŏl (reigned 654 to 660), also seems to indicate some Taoist influence, since scholars relate it to the *Tao te Ching* (Chapter 55), in which the child is depicted as having neither judgment nor desires.[36]

There exists a tile with a mountain view of Packche, depicting three sacred mountains, a Taoist temple and a Taoist monk, all related to the notion of the Taoist immortal. If it is true that these parallels can be drawn, then it follows that Packche knew not only philosophical but also religious Taoism.

Some of the important characteristics of Packche Taoism were introduced to Japan.

Japanese records reveal that Wang In, who introduced the Chinese system of writing to Japan, also knew of the way of Tao.[37] According to the *Nihon shoki (Records of Ancient Matters),* the Packche monk Ganjin came to Japan in the tenth year of the Empress Suiko, 602 A.D., bringing with him calendars, as well as books of divination, Chinese medicine, and astronomy, all of which are considered to have an especially close relation with Taoism.[38]

C. Silla: Exactly when Taoism entered Silla seems somewhat uncertain, however, it is known that King Pŏphŭng (514-539 A.D.) introduced Confucianism, Buddhism and Taoism, with their various cultures from China. Ch'oe Ch'i-wŏn suggests that Silla adopted at this time "a mystical way",[39] which seems to have come from the *Tao-te Ching*. It was called *"feng-liu"*[40] and may be described as poetic refinement. This was a synthesis of the ideas of Confucianism, Buddhism and Taoism.

In practice *feng-liu* (Korean-pŏnglu) adopted filial piety and loyalty to the nation from Confucianism; a "laissez faire" attitude from Taoism and the Buddhist way best described, or expressed, by the axiom "do no evil and do good."

The institution of *Hwarang* (lit. flower-knight) that developed in Silla also combined various activities and beliefs that seem to have had a Taoist origin along with Buddhism and Confucianism. The *Hwarang* was a kind of educational and social institute for young men who met as a group to learn Buddhistic, Confucian and Taoist classics, military techniques, and to enjoy such activities as singing, dancing; games, and visiting mountains. The *Hwarang* also performed a ceremony utilizing elements of magic to communicate with spirits perhaps reflecting shaman practice. In national crises the *Hwarang* was mobilized into a youth corps within the army.[41]

One scholar notes that the *Hwarang* called their meeting-place the "Place of the Four Immortals" which appears to be influenced by Chinese Taoist literature. Moreover, at their meeting-places they carried out rituals to worship the immortals.[42]

We are also told that the great general and member of the *Hwarang*, Kim Yusin, once went to a mountain seeking the protection of the spirits. He disciplined himself through meditation for several days, after which he received inspiration for a unique way to defeat his enemies.[28] This story bears a similarity to one about a Chinese hero, Chang Yung, who received similar inspiration from mystical spirits, on military tactics which enabled him to score a victory,[43] and may have been inspired by the Taoist immortal which appeared as Ch'ŏn'gun, a heavenly being transformed into an old man. Furthermore, General Kim Yusin appears in a legend about the dipper and the sword, something which also seems to be related to Chinese Taoist influence. [44] The legend linked the shamanistic symbol of the sword with the stars, and on the sword, was found the symbol of the dipper. It is evident that in Korea there was a relationship between the magical aspects of shamanism and the dipper symbol as it appears in Taoist thought. [45]

According to the *Samguk sagi,* [46] King Muyŏl (654-660 A.D.) who had earlier travelled to China for diplomatic purposes, read the *Tao te Ching,* and many other Korean students who were studying China seem to have studied Taoist texts. Because many of them came from a low bone-rank, they could not hold high office and as a result retreated to nature, wrote poems, and followed Taoist practices.

Even in the highest realms of politics, however, Taoism was often encouraged, and largely for political motives—the desire for support, and friendly relations with China. Moreover, there is ample evidence that Taoism influenced Silla literature. For example, the *Song of Tosol* or "Flower Mountain" seems to express the mystical and transcendental aspects of Taoism. [48] Also, Ch'ŏyŏng's story of non-violence is an example of Taoism and of the dancing aspect of shamanism brought into synthesis. [49] Okpogo, who wrote *Kŏmun'go,* and the famous kayagŭm-player Uruk, were both called sŏn-in (Taoist hermit). [50] Another example may be the Ch'ŏmsŏngdae, the oldest observatory of East Asia which was built in Silla, since the observation of the stars is related to foretelling the future, often an evidence of Taoist influence.

Yi Nŭng-hwa makes the point that Kim Yusin's grandson and Chang Yang's grandson were considered pioneers in the techniques of the Taoist occult arts. [51]

What seems clear from the above is that the people of the Silla Kingdom read the Taoist scriptures and some, at least, practised techniques of perennial youth and of immortality. It seems equally clear that Taoism came to be blended with shamanism and some aspects of Buddhism, and the synthesis seems to have become the popular religion of Silla. For this reason, Korean history makes mention of the popularity of Taoism in the Silla Kingdom: "the heavenly dragon pleased the people and things were peaceful."[52]

C. Koryŏ: Uniting the later three kingdoms, Wang Kŏn (918-43 A.D.) became the founder of Koryŏ. Among other measures, he handed down ten rules of political direction to be followed by his successors, and in one of them he suggested the holding of the *P'algwan'hoe* festival.[53]

The *P'algwan-hoe* originated in Silla and seems to be connected with the Buddhist religious service, called *Yŭkjil,* which involved abstinence of the part of the laity. Sŏnhae-ko, a Koguryŏ monk, initiated this connection when he came to Silla and established the *P'algwan-hoe.* It became in time a ceremonial festival to honour fallen heroes.[54]

As a new seven-day festival, it was in effect the antithesis of the Buddhist festival it replaced. Instead of one day of abstinence from killing, stealing, sexual relations, ill words, music, dancing, and all work including household duties, there was singing, feasting, dancing and drinking throughout the night. The ceremonial aspects of the festival involved worship of the heavenly spirits of famous mountains, or great rivers, and of dragon gods.[55] It was about this time, the eighth century, that Silla was successful in uniting Koguryŏ and Packche under its rule and forming the new state of Koryŏ. The first king of Koryŏ instituted this newly-evolved Taoist festival as a regular mid-winter event.

As time passed, other elements were added to the *P'algwan-hoe* festival. Along with singing and dancing, sports became a part of the celebration, and competitions were held in which combatants tried to defeat each other by throwing water and stones. The form of combat making use of the empty hand, (rather than the arms as in wrestling), which in Japan was known as karate, and in China as *kung-fu,* was further developed. Fencing and archery were also given encouragement in this new environment, and worship of heavenly spirits, the five great mountains, rivers and dragons, which were naturalistic aspects of Taoist worship, seem to have been added as well.

King T'aejo seems to have believed that the blessing of the Buddha had bestowed upon him the kingship of Koryŏ, and that the special favour of other Buddhist deities had blessed his birthplace of Kaesŏng. He is also said to have believed in "the theory of wind, and flowing water, and earth" divination techniques which were related to Taoism.[56] Thus, he elevated his hometown into a capital city, and also believed that P'yŏngyang was an auspicious site. Honam, the southwestern part of Korea, was regarded as a "place of betrayal", and thus no government officials from there could be appointed.[57] He decreed that Buddhist temples should be built in favorable locations,[39] and the Buddhist monk, Myoch'ŏng, was thus emboldened to request the movement of the capital from Kaesŏng to P'yŏngyang for the prosperity of the nation.[58]

At the beginning of the 13th century, Emperor Hui-tsung of the northern Sung dynasty sent Taoists to establish a shrine in the Koryŏ Kingdom which was, at that time, a tributary state, and the Taoists were welcomed in Koryŏ. The shrine was built near the royal palace, both for the convenience of royalty and for the holding of national religious services in which heaven, earth, mountains, and rivers were all worshipped. On this occasion, as well, a Taoist priest prayed to the gods.[59]

The Koryŏ kings continued to worship the Taoist deities Yuan-shen, Tien-shen and Shan-hsing, but they also revered the planet Mercury and worshipped it as the protector of the family. Even at the present time, many Buddhist temples in Korea have a "hall of the planet Mercury". The purpose of this worship was to seek the blessings of long life, prosperity and having sons as well as to drive away evil spirits and to bring good fortune to the nation. In actual practice, both religions were followed as persons of all classes came to pray at the Taoist temple called Pokwŏn'gwan.[60]

Korean priests modified Chinese external patterns of priesthood to conform more closely to Korean life. Korean Taoist priests wore white clothes, as opposed to the dark blue worn by their Chinese counterparts. Korean priests returned to private homes each evening, whereas Chinese priests usually remained in the temple.[61]

During the reign of King Injŏng (1122-1146 A.D.), there are

several instances of Taoist temple-building. For instance, a temple
called P'alsŏng-dang (pantheon) was built within the palace compound
in P'yŏngyang.[62] This temple was used for general worship and in it,
three images were arranged side by side: one of a shamanistic
mountain god, one of a Taoist deity, and a third of a bodhisattva. They
were regarded as gods of defense and worshippers invoked their
assistance in the national well-being.[63]

At the same time, the beginnings of certain hygenic practices
connected with the Taoist cult of longevity were understood and
practiced by Buddhist monks.[64] Koryŏ ceramics are thought by some to
be greatly influenced by the nihilistic and naturalistic aspects of
Taoism,[65] and indeed, subsequent Korean arts and attitudes continued
to be strongly influenced.

D. Yi Dynasty (1392-1910): The Yi dynasty rose in protest against
the corruption of Koryŏ, and it soon adopted Confucianism as the state
philosophy and religion. T'aejo, the founder of the dynasty, may have
been a practitioner of Taoism but because of the force of the new state
ideology, he did not hesitate to persecute the Taoist church, closing
many. He did, however, allow the Sogyŏkchŏn temple to remain,
along with its staff of about fifteen Taoist priests. In this temple, the
heavenly deities were worshipped on the upper altar, Lao Tzu on the
middle one, and Yama (the lord of Hell) was worshipped on the
lowest. The Sogyŏkchŏn was used to pray for rain, for seeking
blessings, for curing the sick, etc. In addition, he erected the so-called
Sunjedan (the altar of star worship) where ceremonies were carried
out in honour of Taebak (the leviathon) and Kimsŏng (the golden
star). Also, when he moved the capital city to Seoul, he decided to
consult a Taoist fortune-teller about it.[66]

Later, King Sejŏng built the Samsŏngsa for the three Korean
ancestral emperors. There the people came to worship to obtain
longevity and good health, a custom which lasted until late in the
dynasty. It should be noted that in Seoul there still exists a hamlet
called Samch'ŏng-dong which is under Taoist influence and which
worships Taoistic deities such as Taesang lo kun and Kwanje.[67]

In King *Chung jong's* reign (1506-1544), a minister of the

government, the radical Confucian Cho Kwangjo, opposed the institution of the Taoist temple, Sogŏgjŏn, and had it closed. Although it was
subsequently reopened, it was burned in the Imjin conflict with Japan
in the late sixteenth century and was never rebuilt.[68]

II. Characteristics of Taoism
in Modern Korean Culture

In spite of the virtual disappearance of Taoist temples from Korea,
and despite the fact that it was never a strongly-organized religion,
Taoism continues to exist as a "people's religion", along with shamanism, through its influence on other religions and in the popular culture
of modern Korea is not great.

Shamanistic Taoism was practiced by scholars who left Confucianism because of sectarian strife or who failed to pass the
Confucian government examinations. They were people who gathered
together, enjoyed nature and amused themselves together, discussed
Taoistic magic, and left behind them stories of a life of transcendence.

Scholars who had particularly strong Taoist tendencies, criticised
the conservative aspects of Confucianism, instead, developing important historical views. In the seventeenth century, through such books
as *Kyuwŏn Sahwa*,[69] they developed a nationalistic philosophy derived
from the Taoist-Shamanistic view of the Tan'gun myth. This book was
a very significant one because it was opposed to the tendency of
Confucian scholars to worship Chinese superiority. Instead, it uses
the Tan'gun legend to illustrate the high level of *Tongi* (Korean)
civilization.

The *Kyuwŏn Sahwa* also states that Korea from the beginning,
was a country of gentlemen who practiced the theory of non-action
through the eight articles,[70] and claims that the origin of East Asian
civilization is found in the Taoist Tan'gun myth.[51] This work, as
interpreted by the Korean historian Choi Nam-sŏn, suggests the view
that the ancient Korean Shamanistic idea of *Sinsŏn* (divine ascetic)
was even an influence in the development of Chinese Taoism. Other
scholars point out, however, that the *Kyuwŏn Sahwa* seems to

emphasize too strongly a Korea-centric historical view and thus lacks historical objectivity.

Taoistic medicine and certain techniques for ensuring long-life existed even before the Han dynasty in China and in the Korean work called *Tong'ŭi Pogam (Chinese and Korean Medical Writings)* published in 1613, all manner of sicknesses and diseases and their cures were described. In spite of its sophistication, the book includes several sections describing Taoist techniques designed to achieve immortality. Additionally, *Tanhak* became popular, and even though it helped to promote superstition, it also helped to build a Taoist system of medicine. From the seventeenth century onwards, training was offered in such Taoist arts as the cultivation of mind and body, control of health, and refinement of life.

Even well-known Confucian scholars such as T'oegye and Yulgok developed and wrote about the techniques for the preservation of one's health, and with numerous others, are known to have studied Taoist texts and to have written commentaries on them. [71]

Shamanistic Taoism seems to have influenced very considerably people's ideas of how to gain blessings and avoid evils, such as sickness. It was thought for instance, that a blind shaman could cure sickness by repeating scriptures, by using the name of the god on the door of the sickroom, and by beating drums. It was also believed that sickness could be controlled by putting pictures of divinities—like soldiers dressed in gold costumes, or Taoist immortals, on the door of the sickroom, along with Taoist mystical writings.

Divine powers could be secured by avoiding cooked food and having five meals a day. This power could also be borrowed by practising the martial arts. The use of drums and prayer were other avenues by which these powers could be acquired. A person having gained these mystical powers is said to be capable of stopping a car with two fingers, changing a stone to powder, travelling a thousand miles in a night, or even calling forth a butterfly in the middle of winter. Such people become immortal and ascend to heaven from where they are capable of returning when needed by the people. This idea was projected into a kind of hero-worship, and the idea of a god-general who could come back and destroy the enemy (usually the Japanese).[72]

Buddhist monks also practised Taoist divination (such as the reading of Okch'ukung. They were trained in the Taoist martial arts and during the Yi dynasty they contributed to the war effort against Japan.

Most of the new Korean religions, of about the last hundred years, including *Ch'ondo-gyo, Chinch'ŏn-gyo, Poch'ŏn-gyo,* and *Paek pae-gyo,* are all derivations of Taoistic Shamanism. They embrace such concepts as Tao, Lao Tzu, and Tan'gun.

The word *"Ch'ŏndo"* in *Ch'ŏndo-gyo* has the same meaning as Taoism,[73] and Ch'oe Che-wu, the founder of this religion reportedly received the eternal Tao from the heavenly being, the Taoist emperor-God.[74]

Although the modern Korean religion of Ch'ondo-gyo claims to be a synthesis of Confucianism, Buddhism, and Taoistic Shamanism, with possibly some Christian influence, it is, in fact, overwhelmingly grounded in Taoistic Shamanism. From Confucianism they have used the concept of the *chun-tzu* (Gentleman); from Buddhism, the concept of *Hwa-yen* (one is many—many is one) as well as defense of the nation which came from the concept of the pure land on earth. From Christianity they have the ideas of equality and social justice. However, the strongest and most important influence is from Taoism.

Ch'ŏndo-gyo's emphasis on *Mu-wi-Ihwa* appears to be a direct influence from Wu-wei naturalism, which expresses the idea of "being done without doing", a reference to the teaching of Tao.[75] The "man as God" idea of Ch'ŏndo-gyo is drawn from the monistic view of Taoism. Moreover, Ch'ŏndo-gyo stresses that if one receives religious amulets, all sickness can be cured and long life assured, and if, by chanting, one enters a trance, creative power is given. Ch'oe even claimed that he would become *Sinsŏn* (a Taoist deity) and ascend to heaven to receive guidance and creative power which would enable him to stop the Japanese. This idea was set forth in the official song of the faith.

In the Tonghak rebellions (1876-77, 1888-89), which started with non-violent protests against the government, the adherents of the

Ch'ŏndo-gyo finally took up arms when provoked by severe government reaction, and later in March of 1919, they joined with Korean Christians to unite the country against Japanese colonial rule. These actions provide a good illustration of Shamanistic-Taoist living, with non-violence as its Taoist component and with dynamism as its Shamanistic one.

Taoistic Shamanism, however, is not restricted in its strong influence to Ch'ŏndo-gyo, but is also important as an influence in other new religions in Korea. Such concepts of God as Lao Tzu's or that of Tan'gun, some magical elements, the cure of sickness, secular blessings, etc., are to be found in various new religions. This was, perhaps, inevitable, because these elements were at the very root of popular religion and culture from early times.

It should also be noted that those new religions which found their origins in Christianity seem as well to have been greatly influenced by Taoistic-Shamanism. For example, the Rev. Yongdo Yi's Christ-centered mysticism, which was characterised by erotic elements, seems to have been influenced by the *Yin-yang* principles so prominent in Taoism, and the same principles also seem to have influenced Pak Taesun's "Evangelical Hall Movement", and Moon Sŏng-myŏng's Unification Church movement. For example, Pak's curing of sickness and driving out of devils by the laying on of hands show Christian influence, while the practice of using water for the curing of illness is a direct influence of Chinese Taoism. Moon's Unification Church seems to have been influenced by the *Yin-yang* principle for sexual relations, which in turn was an influence from Yi Yŏngdo (1901-1933).[76] When Moon conducts communal marriages, he puts on a "dipper crown", borrowing symbolism from both Taoism and Shamanism.

Korean Taoism as noted above, was always prominent in poetry, literature, and the arts, and there exist several good studies of this subject.[77]

The paintings of the Yi dynasty often had as their subjects, nature and animals, which would seem to be Taoistic, but on closer examination, they show a good deal of shamanistic influence. For example, "year pictures" were painted in the royal palace, and their subjects were stars, fairy ladies, the sun, divine generals, and especially the ten "long-life" symbols along with abstract tigers and roosters.[78]

Korean Taoism, which can more accurately be described as Shamanistic Taoism, occupied the place of a state religion in Koguryŏ, Pakche and Silla until they were united by Koryŏ.

Taoism was incorporated into Korea in a systematic fashion and thus it influenced the thinking and practices of the people, but in spite of this, Taoism was never organized to the same degree as Buddhism.

The idea of harmonization in Taoistic Shamanism emerged in *Hwarangdo* and *Ch'ŏndo-gyo,* as well as in new religions uniting Confucianism, Buddhism and even Christianity. Also, the influence of Korean Taoism extended to Hŏ Chun's *Tong'ŭi Pogam*—Taoist medicine and the technique developed for the preservation of health— the Neo-Confucianist concept of energy, developed by Yulgok and the "dipper hall" which existed in Buddhist temples.

Taoism was also expressed through poetry, literature, and especially the unique Korean ceramics and abstract arts, known as *Minhwa.* Korean Taoism bears a close resemblance to the religious practices of Japan, and comparision of both would shed more light on the common spiritual and cultural foundations shared by both countries.

My own research has led me to disagree with the views of some specialists in Asian religion who suggest Buddhism as the common ground for the religions of China, Korea and Japan. Instead it appears to me that since Shamanistic Taoism was more common to the experience of the masses, it would more likely comprise the basis of the people's religion and culture in these three countries. Even in Christianity the concept of God and the mystical dynamic of the religion appeal to Korean thought since they strike a common note with Shamanistic Taoism. It is the peculiar circumstances of Korea that have led to a closer connection and growth of Christianity in Korea than in either China and Japan.

I have hoped to clarify, in this brief sketch, the often misleading impression that Taoism has not been a major element of the Korean religious experience, because it is not immediately noticeable by imposing temple complexes or other monuments. We would do well to direct more attention to cross-cultural influences between religions, rather than to the institutionalized forms, based as they are on more fundamental concerns of all Asian religion: mystical experience, cyclical change, and natural phenomena.

Endnotes

1. Yi, Nŭng-Hwa, *Han'guk togyo so* (History of Korean Taoism), Tongkuk Univ. 1959. Some Articles on Korean Taoism. Koba N, "Chosen no Tokyo (On Taoism in Korea)". *Tōhōgaku* (Eastern Studies), ed. The Institute of Eastern Culture, No. 29. Feb. 1965. Also articles on Korean Taoistic Studies included in *Han'guk Ch'ŏrnakhoe Han'guk Ch'ŏrhak Yŏn'gu* (A Study of Korean Philosophy), Vol. I, II, III.

2. Generally, the introduction to Korean religions is not treated or included as a separate chapter. For example: Kim, Tŭk-hwang *Han'guk Chonggyosa* (Religious History of Korea), Seoul: Haemun Sa, 1963, Minjok Munhwa Yŏn-guso, ed., *Han'guk munhwasa taege* VI (Outline of Korean Culture VI), Chonggyo Ch'ŏrhaksa (History of Religion and Philosophy), Seoul: Minjok munhwa yŏnguso, Korea Univ. 1964-70. Wongwang Univ. ed., *Han'guk chonggyo* (Korean Religion), Wongwang Univ. Press, 1973.

3. *Samguk Sagi* (History of the Three Kingdoms), *Samguk Yusa* (Legends and History of the Three Kingdoms of Ancient Korea), *Yijo sillok* (The Veritable Records of the Yi Dynasty), Ch'ŏngsa (prayers written on blue paper—a Taoist religious custom), *Kyuwŏn Sa Hwa* (An Historical Tale of Kyuwon). Incantations recorded in individual anthologies.

4. Koba, op. cit., pp. 118-119.

5. Han Yŏng-u. "Sip ch'il segi ŭi pan, chonhwajŏk toga sahak ŭi sŏngjang" ("The growth of the opposition to Chinese Taoism in the 17th century") *Han'guk ŭi yŏksa insik* (Historical Consciousness of Korea) (Vol. 1), p. 282.

6. Iryŏn, *Samguk Yusa* (Legends and History of the Three Kingdoms of Ancient Korea), tr. T'ae-hung Ha, Grafton K. Mintz, Yonsei Univ. Press, Seoul, 1972, pp. 32-33.

7. Yi, Kibaek, *Han'guk kodae saron* (An Essay on Ancient Korean History), T'am gu dang, Seoul, 1977, p. 14.

8. Shih Chi, Vol. 6. Cf. Yi Nŭng-hwa *Han'guk togyosa* (History of Korean Taoism). Tongkuk University Press, 1959, pp. 40-43.

9. Cf. Kubo, pp. 120-121.

10. Kim, Pu-sik, *Samguk Sagi* (History of the Three Kingdoms of Ancient Korea), tr. in Korean by Yi Pyŏng-do, Ulyu mun-hwa sa, Seoul, 1977, p. 710 cf. Iryŏn, *Samguk Yusa* (History and Legends of the Three Kingdoms of Ancient Korea), tr. in English, Yonsei Univ. Press, 1972, pp. 193-194.

11. Kobo, M. op. cit., pp. 122-123 cf. *Nihon Shoki* (History of Japan, A.D..).

12. An Pyŏngju, "Koguryŏ ŭi togyo Sasange Kwanhayŏ" (About Koguryŏ Taoistic Thought), *A Study of Korean Philosophy* Vol. I. Ibid., p. 303.

13. *Samguk Yusa*, op. cit., pp. 33-35.

14. Cha, Juwhan, "Koguryŏ ŭi togyo sasang" (Taoistic Thought of Koguryŏ), *Han'guk Ch'ŏrhak Yŏn-gu* Vol. I (A Study of Korean Philosophy, Vol. I), pp. 294-295.

15. Cf. Kim, Wŏnyong, *Koguryŏ misul* (Arts of Koguryŏ), *Han'guk sasang ch'ongsŏ* (Series of Korean Thought, Vol. I), Han'guk sasang Yŏngu Hoe, 1973, pp. 130-139.

16. *Samguk Yusa*, pp. 193-194.

17. Ibid.

18. Cf. Kubo Ibid., p. 122, Cho Ibid., p. 290.

19. Ilyŏn op. cit., pp. 193-194, Cha op. cit., pp. 289-290.

20. Cf. Kubo, op. cit., p. 122, Cho, op. cit., pp. 282- 285.

21. Cha op. cit., p. 283.

22. Song Hang-yong, "Koguryŏ ŭi togyo sasang ŭl ilkko" (Reading About Koguryŏ Taoistic Thought), *Han'guk Ch'ŏrhak Yŏn-gu,* p. 298.

23. Cf. Iryŏn op. cit., pp. 193-194, Cha, op. cit., p. 292.

24. Ibid., pp. 281-282.

25. Iryŏn Ibid., pp. 45-47, Cha, op. cit., pp. 279-281.

26. Ibid., p. 280.

27. Ibid.

28. Ibid.

29. Cho Chihun, *Han'guk munhwasa sosŏl* (Introduction to Korean Civilization) T'amgu dang Seoul 1964, p. 97.

30. Cha. Ibid., p. 376.

31. Cho, op. cit., p. 97.

32. Ling-hu, Te-fen, *Chou shu* vol. 3. Chunghua Press, Peking, p. 887.

33. *Samguk Sagi,* op. cit., p. 376.

34. Ibid., p. 401.

35. Ibid., pp. 423-424.

36. Kim, Kumyŏng *Munyŏng wang nŭng,* (Royal Tomb of King Muyŏl). Kendo, Tokyo, 1983, pp. 65-66.

37. Yi, Nŭng-hwa, op. cit., pp. 55-56.

38. Op. cit. Cf. *Nihon Shoki* Vol. 22

19. *Samguk Sagi,* ibid. p. 62.

40. Cf. *Tao te Ching,* Chapter 1.

41. Cha, Ibid., pp. 344-345.

42. Cha, Ibid.

43. Yi, Nung-hwa, op. cit., pp. 94-98.

44. *Samguk Yusa,* op. cit., p. 77.

45. Ch'a Chuhwan, op. cit., pp. 350-351. cf. *Samguk Sagi,* op. cit., pp. 147-148, cf. Cha.

46. Ch'a Chu-hwan, *Silla sa Hoe wa togyo sasang* (Silla Society and Taoistic Thought).

47. *Han'guk Ch'ŏrhak Yŏngu* Vol. I. op. cit., pp. 337-338. Ibid., pp. 353-354.

48. Yi Nŭng-hwa, op. cit., pp. 98-100. Cf. *Samguk Yusa,* op. cit., p. 352, "Wolmyŏng then improvised a 'Tosol-ga' (Song of the Tushita Heaven) as follows:
    I sing as I scatter thee, Oh flowers!
    Fall and obey the decree of a straight mind;
    Attend the King Maitreya on his throne."

49. Op. cit., p. 127.
"Under the moonlight of the Eastern Capital
I revelled late into the night.
When I came home and entered my bedroom
I saw four legs. Two legs are mine,
To whom to the other two belong? The person
Below me is mine, but whose body is raping her?
What shall I do? Thus he sang and danced . . . ."

50. Ch'a Chu-hwan, op. cit., pp. 346-347.

51. Yi Nŭng-hwa, op. cit., p. 97.

52. *Koryŏ sa* Vol. 18.

53. Pae, Chong-ho, *Koryŏ ŭi togyo sasang (Taoist Thought of Koryŏ), Hanguk Ch'ŏrhak hak sasang* Vol. I. ibid. p. 366, cf. Son, Po-ki, *The History of Korea*, Korean National Commission for UNESCO, Seoul, Korea, 1970, p. 100.

54. Lee Nŭng-hwa, op. cit., pp. 98-100.

55. Cf. Cha op. cit., 340-345.

56. Han U-gŭn, *The History of Korea*. The Eul-yoo Publishing Co., 1970, p. 125-126.

57. Ibid.

58. Ibid.
59. Yi, Nŭng-hwa, op. cit., pp. 137-138.

60. Pae Chong ho "Koryŏ ŭi togyo sasang (The Thought of Koryŏ Taoism)" *Han'guk Ch'orhak Yŏn'gu* pp. 375.

61. Lee Nŭng-hwa, op. cit., pp. 116-119.

62. Ibid., pp. 101-102.

63. Ibid.

64. Ibid., pp. 144-145.

65. Because of the Mongolian invasion and the trouble brought to Koryŏ by the Kitan, and furthermore, because of military government control, the people of Koryŏ suffered greatly and had not much hope of happiness in their earthly life. Because of these circumstances the Koryŏ people seem to have been nihilistic and to have followed a naturalistic life style. This was expressed through Koryŏ ceramics, which seem to have been influenced by Zen Buddhism and Taoism.

66. cf. Ch'a, Chu-hwan, "Chosŏn Cho Chŏn gi ŭi togyo sasang (Taoist Thought of Early Yi Dynasty)," *Han'guk Ch'orhak Yŏn'gu* Vol. II. pp. 101-106.

67. cf. Yi, Nŭng-Hwa, op. cit., pp. 181-187.

68. Ch'a, Chu-hwan op. cit., p. 101.

69. cf. Han, Yŏng-Wu, op. cit., pp. 263-305.

70. Ibid. cf. Han, Yŏng-u, Ibid. p. 21, cf. Yi, Pyŏng-do, *Kuksa taegwan* (General Survey of Korean History), Pomun Sa, Seoul, Korea, 1955, pp. 34-37.

71. cf. *Yulgok Chŏnjip*, Taedong Munhwa Yŏngu wŏn, Seoul. *Han'guk Ch'orhak Yŏn'gu*, Vol. III. p. 103.

72. Cho, Chi-Hun, "Han'gu ŭi chong gyo wa kŭ paegyŏng (Korean Religion and Its Background)," "Hyŏndae in Kang-jwa (Essays on Modernists)," Pak Mun Sa, Seoul, 1962, p. 306.

73. Takeuchi, Yoshio, *Chukoku sisoshi* (A History of Chinese Thought), Iwanami Shoten, Tokyo, 1967, p. 46.

74. Kim Yong Choon *The Ch'ŏndogyo Concept of Man.*Pan Korea Book Corporation, Seoul, p. 78.

75. Ibid., pp. 15-16.

76. Min Kyŏng-pae *Kyohoe wa minjok (Church and Race)*, Seoul, 1981, pp. 285-288.

77. Cf. Yi, Chong-ŭn, *Han'guk siga sang ŭi togyo sasang* Yŏn'gu (A Study of Taoism in Korean Poems), Posŏng Mun Hwa Sa, Seoul, 1978, pp. 175-181.

78. cf. Zo, Za-Yong, "A Note on Korean Folk Paintings", *Aspects of Korean Culture*, Su Do Women's Teachers College Press, Seoul, 1974, pp. 209-223.

Regional Characteristics of Shamanism in Korea

1. Introduction

The purpose of this study is to explore the characteristics of Korean Shamanism and its regional variations. The basic materials used were collected through fieldwork in South Korea between 1960 and 1982. Travel to North Korea was not possible due to the political situation, therefore northern shamanistic practices were derived by studying the shamans of northern origin. In addition, previous research reports were also utilized. I have confined my study to the development of shaman practices, the Korean perception of gods, and a religio-folkloric perspective on shamanistic rituals.

As of December, 1975, more than fifty thousand shamans were affiliated with the Korean Anti-Communist Worshipping Association. Assuming that there are many who do not join the association because of the monthly membership dues and that there are many who are not legitimate shamans but either fortune-tellers or physiognomists, this figure should be regarded as a rough estimate.

Based on nation-wide field—work the following regional samples were selected: twelve sites in the Chungbu Region (Central Korea), seven in the Yŏngdong Region (Mid-Eastern Korea), fourteen in the Honam Region (South-Western Korea), ten in the Yŏn-nam Region (Southeastern Korea), two on Cheju Island, one in the Haesoe Region (Mid-Western Korea), one in the Kwan-sŏ Region (North-Western Korea), for a total of forty-eight regions. From these, seven sample cases were selected to be used in this study: three in central Korea (one in Seoul, one in Ch'ung-ch'ŏng Province, one in the Yŏngdong Region), one in Honam, one in Yŏngnam, one on Cheju Island, and one from the Kwanbuk, Kwansŏ, and Haesŏ Regions.

Types of Shamans and their Regional Distribution

According to the data collected, there are four types of shamans in Korea: A. *mudang,* B. *tan'gol,* C. *simbang,* and D. *myŏngdu.*

In the *mudang* type, one becomes a shaman through a process called *kang-sin ch'e-hŏm,* which means "experiencing a descent of the shaman spirit", which often follows a serious illness. The *mudang* may officiate at ritualistic occasions with songs and dances, and is able to tell fortunes through the spiritual power of a deity. Along with the *'paksu'* (the male *mudang*) and the so-called *sŏn-mudang* such as *posal, ch'i 'sŏng halmŏm,* pŏpsa, etc. the *mudang*-type can be found both in central and northern Korea. Although the sŏn-mudangs have spiritual power acquired through *kang-sin ch'e-hŏm* they are shamans of lower rank who cannot perform rituals with a complete knowledge of song and dance. Their function is restricted to performing *pison,* simple rituals and fortune-telling. Their range may sometimes extend into southern Korea and Cheju Island.

The *sŏn-mudangs* are named after the titles of the gods by whom they are possessed along with the suffix *"halmŏm"* (old woman); so *sinjang halmŏm* is an individual possessed by the *sinjang* god and *ch'ilsŏng halmŏm* by the *ch'ilsŏng* god. The *posal shaman* has a Buddhist flavour, worshipping *posal* as the *momju* god and setting up a Buddhist altar. Although this type (Bodhisattva) of *bosal* shaman has spiritual power acquired through *kang-sin-ch'e-hŏm,* she is not able to officiate at rituals with song and dance, but only performs simple rituals. The *pupsa,* unable to officiate at legitimate rituals for the same reason, perform rituals by *toggyŏng* (reading Buddhist and Taoist scriptures). If this type of shaman is illiterate, she calls in a professional sūtra reader, and only receives shamanistic messages. This type of ritual, which only needs the sūtra reading, the drum sounds, and the sitting shaman, is called the 'sitting-ritual'. Rites performed mainly by song and dance while the shaman remains standing, are called 'standing-rituals' and are frequently found in Ch'ung-ch'ŏng Province.

The tan'gol-type shaman is created by inheriting *"sajegwŏn"* (priestly authority), which means the authority of officiating at rituals, and this is passed from generation to generation. Certain jurisdictional areas, based on shamanistic traditions and the priesthood controlling them, are transferred according to institutionalized descent. The *tan'gol* in the Honam region and the *'mudang'* of Yŏngnam region are of this type. The *tan'gol* has a certain jurisdiction of her own, which is called *'tan'gol p'an'* and establishes the collective relationship of the shamanistic followers within that jurisdiction.

The *Simbang*-type, like the *tan'gol*-type, is an hereditary shaman who inherits *sajegwŏn*. The *simbang,* found on Cheju Island, show an institutionalized aspect of shamanistic tradition and an established view of the gods, emphasizing spiritual power. In this, they differ from the *tan'gol*-type who lack any conscious faith in the gods. They differ, too, from the *mudang*-type since they seek the god's will through divination rather than by being directly possessed by the spirit of the god. The *simbang*-type is distinct from both the *tan'gol* and the *mudang*-types, and may be seen as occupying the middle position between the two. However, being unable to directly receive the oracle of the god, and having their major function in officiating at rituals, they are more closely related to the *tan'gol*-type.

The *'myŏngdu'* type of shaman originates from *kangsin ch'ehŏm,* which means receiving the spirit of a dead person. The spirit possessing the *myŏngdu* shaman is that of a dead child, usually under the age of seven, occasionally near the age of sixteen, with some claim to kinship with the shaman. The spirit of the dead child is enshrined in the family shrine and is called for by the shaman to divine the future. The spirit of a female child is called *'myŏngdu'* and that of a male child *'tongja'* or *'taeju'*. The shaman is called by the same name as that of the spirit possessing him. This type of shaman is found mostly in the Honam region and also in central and northern Korea. The *myŏngdu* shamans used to specialize in divination but have lately taken to officiating at rituals, thereby coming into conflict with the *tan'gol* shamans.

Apart from categorizing the shamans of Korea into the *mudang, tan'gol, simbang,* and *myŏngdu* types, they can be further classified into two distinct categories: the *mudang* and the *myŏngdu* types as *'kangsin* shamans' (charismatic) and the *tan'gol* and *simbang* types as hereditary shamans (priestly). The *kangsin* shamans are found largely in central and northern Korea, while the hereditary shamans are confined mainly to the southern part of the country.

2. Shaman Practice in Central and Northern Korea

The view of the gods is determined by *'sŏngmu kwajŏng* (the process of becoming a shaman) and differing views of the gods create the features of the rituals. The regional characteristics of shaman practice will be explored with these in mind.

1) *Sŏngmu kwajŏng* and the "View of the Gods"

Central and northern parts of Korea are generally the homes of *kangsin* shamans. *Sinbyŏng ch'ehŏm,* which means "experience of mystic illness", is necessary to becoming a *kangsin* shaman, so a brief overview of the symptoms of *kangsin ch'ehŏm* is required.

A mystic illness caused by the spirit of a god usually begins without any clear cause: the individual is unable to eat normally, perhaps developing indigestion or an aversion to meat or fish. She may be reduced to drinking only water, and may experience weight loss, weakness, pains on one side of the body, prolonged periods of hemorrhaging and continual stress. The subject becomes restless and dreams frequently of communication with the god. She becomes unable to distinguish dreams from reality, hallucinating and hearing the god's voice even in a waking state. As the condition progresses she may go mad, and take to wandering around the mountains and the forest. *Sinbyŏng ch'ehŏm* may occasionally first manifest itself with mental disorder but the usual progression is from physical to mental incapacity.

The period of illness is long, from an average of eight years to a maximum of thirty. No medical treatment is possible and the illness is believed to be cured only by *kangsin ch'e,* or "the ritual of the advent of the god". It is believed that the only way to escape the affliction is to become a shaman following the fate revealed by the god. If the shaman gives up the job after a cure has been effected, the illness will recur.

This can be viewed, in religious terms, as a god revealing his will by choosing the person who is to be afflicted, and the hallucinations, experienced in the waking state as well as in dreams, imply the religious experience of a god.

While suffering from such an illness, the afflicted person will go to fortune-tellers to seek its cause and how best to remedy it. If it proves to be a *sinbyŏng,* she must conduct a so-called *naerim-kut* to enshrine the god who has descended into her body. A *naerim-kut* will be conducted by a prominent shaman and she will enshrine the god in the *kangsinja* which means the person who is possessed with the god's spirit. This is called *sŏngmu-ŭisik* or the ritual of becoming a shaman. The *kangsinja* is supposed to tell the name of the god by whom she is possessed at the ritual by picking up one of the bowls on the *sinmyŏng* table, which is a table of the names of the gods. After that the *kangsinja* will jump up and dance violently. It is at this moment that she changes from human to divine and leaves the secular world to enter into the divine one; she becomes a shaman with the authority of the god possessing her. The mysterious illness, the dreaming, the hallucinations and the wanderings all symbolize the death of her secular being, and *naerim-kut* symbolizes her rebirth as a divine entity.

The *kangsinja* enshrines the god in her home and an altar is set up in a *taech'ŏng* room with the paintings of the shaman gods, or a scroll inscribed with their names, hung on the wall. Here she offers sacred water and prays. The *kangsinja* becomes a follower of the shaman who officiated at the *naerim-kut,* and learns to perform the shaman rituals. Their relationship is that of mother and daughter, linked together by the will of the god. The period of apprenticeship, which varies according to individual aptitude, generally lasts for three years, after which the *kangsinja* becomes an independent shaman.

At the beginning, the *kangsinja* attends the shaman rituals and helps the chief shaman by taking care of the necessary instruments and offerings. Sometimes she will play the *chegŭm* (one of the traditional Korean musical instruments). When she becomes familiar with the rhythms of shamanistic songs she will play the *chango* (a drum) and after memorizing the words of the songs she will wear the robe and take part in the simpler procedures of the ritual.

The *kangsinja* sets up an altar at her home with a painting of the god on a shelf below it. If a painting is not available, then the name of the god written on a piece of paper is acceptable until she can obtain a proper painting. The paintings are on scrolls of about 100 cm x 60 cm, painted by an artisan (a *tangchae* or *sŏkch'ae*). The *kangsinja* will usually have the artisan create the painting based on the image of the god she received in her dreams or hallucinations. She will offer sacred water every morning and afternoon along with bowing and praying. The name of the god will be known by the contents of the bowl the *kangsinja* picked up from the *sinmyŏng* table at the *naerim-kut*;

Red bean	*sŏnang*	Tutelary god
Bean	*kunung*	Household god
Rice	*chesŏk*	Indra
Sesame	*san*	Mountain god
Buckwheat	*tuhaju*	House site god
Water	*yŏng*	Dragon
Fodder	*ch'ŏju*	Shaman spirit
Ashes	*puchang*	Purification god.

Generally there will be from fifteen to twenty representations of the different gods including:

sambulchesŏk,	The Three Buddhas and Indra
ch'ilsŏng	The Great Dipper or Seven Stars god
irwŏl sŏng,	The sun, moon, and stars god
sinjang	Divine General
yong	Dragon God
taegam	Officials of the gods
taejo	The founder of Yi dynasty (King as god)

From a vague imagining of the god to a conviction of its actual existence, the *kangsinja* enshrines her experience in the altar, a concrete expression of her belief in the god and, as part of the religious ceremony, she offers sacred water and prayers to it.

The gods of the *kangsin* shamans are hierarchically divided into four ranks; high, middle, low, and lowest.

High	*chunsin, ch'ilsŏng* (The Great Dipper), *irwŏrsŏng* (Sun, moon, and stars gods).
Middle	*sansin* (Mountain gods), *sambul chesŏk* (The Three Buddhas and Indra), *sahae yongsin,* (The Dragon of the Four Seas), *chisin* (The Earth god), *taegamsin* (officials as gods), *sinjang* (The Divine General) and *pugunsin* (District office gods).
Low	*yŏnsan, chapkwi* (Demons).

Each of the gods in shamanism has its own responsibility and when there is discord among them, the people suffer misfortune.

Gods exist, but, like the wind, they have no form. They are almighty in the control of human affairs. They reveal their intentions by speaking through the shaman in such a way as not to harm the people.

2) Rituals and Tools

The rituals of the *kangsin* shaman are based on her faith in the existence of her god. In a ritual, the *kangsin* shaman will be unified with the god and the ritual becomes monistic; that is, the shaman becomes divine rather than articulating prayers as a human to a god. Once the god has possessed the shaman, she is apotheosized and utters the words of the god (*kŏngsu*) to foretell the future. During the ritual, the movements and expressions of the shaman are not those of a human, but those of the god within her. Even the robe she wears implies that she is not human but divine.

The shaman ritual is not a secular routine but a divine occasion. Seven or fifteen days before the ritual, the site of the ceremony is marked off by golden lines and sand is spread on it indicating the restricted area. In this way, the site is separated from the secular world and becomes chaos, the realm of the shaman gods. The ritual takes place at night which belongs to the gods.

The shaman, through her *kangshin-ch'ehŏm,* ends her secular life and returns to the divine chaos to be born again. For this reason, she can always gain entry into the world of the gods.

The tools used by the *kangsin* shaman are related to or symbolize the gods. They include not only the bell, fan, and knife but also such things as robes, musical instruments, and paintings of the gods. *Onwŏlto, samjich'ang,* and *chakdu* symbolize the dignity of the god and are used when the shaman impersonates it. The traditional Korean musical instruments, especially the quick beat of the percussives, such as the *puk, changgo, ching, chegum, p'iri, chŏtdae,* and *haegŭm* help to immerse the shaman in the ritual. The *'ch'ongbae',* or the calling of the god, will be followed by the shaman's dance to the violent beat of the percussion instruments. They are believed to hasten the arrival of the god. The bell is also used to summon the god, and the fan symbolizes the majesty of the god. There are fifteen different kinds of robes that the shamans wear in the Seoul area *Changgun Ch'ima. Changgun Chŏgori, Kugunbok, Chŏnbok, Namch'ŏnik, Hongchŏnik, Pakchangsam, Hŭkchangsam, Pulsaot, Puinot, Ch'angbuot, Shinjangot.* Shamans in Pyongan or Hwanghae province have about twenty to thirty different robes, each for a different ritual. The number of robes a shaman has will be determined by the different types of rituals at which she officiates.

3. Shaman Practices in Southern Korea

1) *Sŏngmu-Kwajŏng* and *Singwan*

The shamans of southern Korea are mainly hereditary ones whose status is transferred through descent from generation to generation.

Sajegwŏn or the authority to officiate at shamanistic rituals is inherited through the paternal line, and the woman who marries the possessor of *sajegwŏn* will become a shaman in her own right. This marriage is called *mugyehon,* that is, a marriage between two shaman families. The male successor of a shaman who has *sajegwŏn* will attend rituals after he is fourteen or fifteen years old to learn how to handle the musical instruments required in the ceremony. He will learn at first to play the *ching* (a percussion instrument made of brass). After mastering *changgo* he will learn *'Kŏri-p'uri'* which is the final part of the ceremony. In the case of the girl who is to be his bride, she begins to learn the words of the shaman music from her mother around the age of ten. Being illiterate she is taught verbally and memorizes the words.

They marry in their late teens and the bride follows her mother-in-law, attending the rituals to learn the shamanistic songs and dances, and the procedures of the ceremonies. She already has the words of the songs taught to her by her mother and learns the melodies and dance motions from her mother-in-law. After an apprenticeship of about three years she is able to officiate at simple rituals. Her mother-in-law will give her the chance to officiate at more important ceremonies so that she may become more independent. When the mother-in-law dies or becomes too old to perform her duties, the daughter-in-law succeeds her. In the Honam region, the succession is through paternal lines based on *tan'golp'an* (hereditary priestly authority). In the Yŏngnam region, the method of succession is the same although the use of *tan'golp'an* has disappeared. The *'sinbang'* (divination) of Cheju Island have the same methods. When the *tan'golp'an* system breaks down, the practice of hereditary shamanism also seems to disappear.

The hereditary shaman, unlike the *kangsin* (charismatic) shaman who has *kangsin ch'ehŏm* (spirit possession), seems to have a very weak belief in the gods. The hereditary shaman does not enshrine any god in her home, having had no direct experience with one. The hereditary shaman tends to see the institutional aspects of the rituals as being more important than the spiritual power of the gods because she officiates at the rituals with inherited authority and not with the spiritual possession of the *kangsin* shaman. No element of a belief in gods is found in the hereditary shaman's rituals; they are performed not because of religious faith but simply because they are traditionally regarded as bringing good luck.

The *'sinbang'* shaman of Cheju Island, although one of the hereditary shamans, seems to see the spiritual power of the gods as being of more significance. She treasures *myŏngdu* and *sanp'an* as spiritual power and in rituals she divinates by asking the god's will with *myŏngdu* and *sanp'an*. Like the *kangsin* shaman, the *sinbang* shaman emphasizes the existence of gods; however, unlike her, the *sinbang* is not directly related to the gods and does not transfer herself over to a god during the rituals. The *sinbang* shaman therefore seems to fall between the hereditary shaman of the Honam or Yŏngnam regions and the *kangsin* shamans of central and northern Korea.

2) Rituals and Implements

The rituals of the hereditary shamans show dualistic characteristics in their relationship with the gods. Unlike the monistic qualities of the *kangsin* shaman who is apotheosized in the rituals, the hereditary shaman conveys the wishes of the people to the god in a face-to-face relationship with it. There is no *'kongsu'* or divination in the ceremonies of the hereditary shamans. The rituals are performed ceremonially without any element of the spiritual power of the shaman. In *'ogigut'*, a ritual of the hereditary shamans of the Yŏngnam region, the shaman dances, violently shaking a *sindaechip* which symbolizes her possession by the spirit of the dead. But this is mainly ceremonial, and differs from the *kangsin* shaman's ritual. Dances of the hereditary shamans of the Honam Region also do not have the same spiritual power as the rituals of the *kangsin* shaman.

Robes generally function as a symbol of the transformation of a shaman into a god but they are of little importance to the hereditary shaman as she is not apotheosized in the rituals. The *tan'gol* shaman in the Honam Region wears the clean white *ch'ima-jŏŏgori* (the traditional Korean women's costume), and only in important rituals will she wear the white *turumagi* (the traditional Korean overcoat) and the *kokkal* (a hat made of white paper). The traditional shaman robes seem almost to have disappeared. In 1969, this writer obtained a shaman robe from a *tan'gol* shaman in Kwang-yang-eup in Chungnam Province who had inherited it from her grandmother. She said that her mother used to wear it at ceremonies for old people. It is believed that the shamans wore robes in the past but that the custom has died out. The hereditary shamans of the Yŏngnam region, the *mudang*, have two kinds of robes, the *k'oeja* and the *hwalot*. The *simbang* and the hereditary shamans of Cheju Island also have only two kinds of robes; the *kwandi* and the *sŏpsu*. That the hereditary shamans of Honam, Yŏngnam region and Cheju Island have few, if any robes indicates that the practice of wearing robes, which is more ceremonial than symbolic of the actual advent of a god, is disappearing.

Many musical instruments are used by the hereditary shamans in their ceremonies. Implements for the ceremonies also include swords and bells; the bells are used to summon the god, and the divine swords are used to soothe the souls of the dead.

Conclusion

The shamans of Korea can be categorized into four types; the *mudang* type of central and northern Korea, the *tan'gol* type of Honam region, the *sinbang* type of Cheju Island, and the *myŏngdu* type of the Honam region. The *mudang* and the *myŏngdu* types are *kangsin* shamans whose spiritual powers are regarded as the major function of their shamanistic practices. The *tan'gol* and the *simbang* types are hereditary shamans who inherit *sajegwŏn* through institutionalized ways and have their main function in officiating at rituals.

Shamans in central and northern Korea who become shamans through *kangsin ch'ehŏm* believe in the existence of gods, and divine the future and perform ceremonies with the spiritual power of the gods by whom they are possessed. Hereditary shamans of Southern Korea, since they become shamans by inheriting *sajegwŏn* do not have spiritual power and their rituals are generally ceremonial functions. Shamans in central and northern Korea have altars enshrining the gods they have experienced, and have a monistic system of rituals, as well as the robes and the tools for such practices. Shamans of southern Korea do not have altars, and with their lack of belief in the gods and with their dualistic system of ceremonies do not have sacred robes or tools imbued with sacred powers. The shaman practice of central and northern Korea can be characterised by its spiritual power, whereas that of the south, by the inheritance of *sajegwŏn* based on the *tan'gol* system. The regional difference in the characteristics of Korean shamanistic practices is believed to be based on the spiritual power which the shaman possesses.

Chart of Types of Korean Shamans

Possession		Hereditary	
Mudang Central and N. Korea	Myŏngdu Honam District	Tan'gol Honam	Sinbang Cheju Island
Possession by descent of a shamanistic spirit (Kang-sin ch'ehŏm)		Priest authority is inherited. (Sajegwŏn)	
Sŏn-mudang named after gods who possess them to which is added the suffix "hal- wŏn" (Old Woman).	Possessed by spirits of the dead: called a myŏngdu if the spirit is female or Tongja if male.	Hereditary	Receives mes- sages through divination.
Possessed perform simple rituals (pison) without knowledge of song and dance.		Hereditary class performs rituals of song and dance.	

Kut and the Treatment of Mental Disorder

I. Introduction

The reason that psychiatry is interested in shamanistic treatment is not only that its rituals seem effective in the treatment of mentally-disordered people but they seem also to elevate such individuals to a state of normally functioning human beings. Accordingly, academic interest focuses on the following areas: how, in shamanistic treatment, the sufferings and anxiety of people are dissolved, how mentally-disordered persons are being treated and thus elevated to a position of contributing members in society, and finally, what kind of effect shamanistic treatment has on the mentality and characteristics of the Korean population in the wider sense.

This author has been able to observe in detail the process of healing by exorcism (*kut*) and analyze the cause and meaning of the disorders which are treated with *kut* through field research during the last four years. In Korea, research on shamanistic treatment has been done mainly by Mr. Puyŏng Yi and myself, with the former basing his work principally on documents and literature using the perspective of Jung's Analytical Psychiatry to define the symbolic meaning of shamanistic treatment. The purpose of this paper, on the other hand, is to describe phenomenologically the present state of Korean shamanistic treatment, discuss the principles of such treatment, and examine, in relation to the mental characteristics of the Korean people, problems that arise out of such treatment.

II. Research Materials and Method

The materials for this paper have been collected by field research in Kyŏnggi-do and the Seoul area over the last four years. Accordingly, they do not cover all the areas in Korea but concentrate on the kangsin (charismatic) type of shamanism of the middle region of Korea, and add to this, some findings based on the *sesŭp* shamanism of Kyŏnggi-do and Chŏlla-do.

The materials on *kut* were gathered by the participation-observation method, by interviewing the patients about their life history, medical history, diagnosis of the disease, and the follow-up of each case for at least one year or more. Therefore, this research neglects document analysis and is limited to case analysis.

III. The General Characteristics of Shamanistic Treatment

The *kut* is performed when a family or a village is faced with an unfortunate event. When disease, natural disaster, accident, or death has occurred, or when the danger of such is imminent, a *kut* is performed. In other words, the *kut* has both curative and preventative functions. However, when the *kut* is performed with an intention of preventing three such disasters, it is carried out to dissolve the fear and anxiety of people who foresee the danger, and thus also has a curative function. However, for the purposes of this paper, the scope of discussion will be limited to the shamanistic ceremonies specifically designed to treat diseases.

The first aspect we will discuss is that of *chŏm* (divination) which resembles the diagnosis of modern medicine. When someone becomes ill, the family of the patient or the patient himself approaches a *mudang* or a *chŏmjaengi* (fortune-teller). At this meeting, a brief report on the patient's sex, birth date and time of birth, medical history, and family will be made. If this information is not fully available, they supply it to the best of their ability. Based on this, the *chŏm* is conducted. There is a variety of techniques, such as the spiritual, the bell, the rice, the coin, the bamboo pipe, the flags, and the turtle divination and one or a combination of more than one are used together. The bell indicates the presence of sickness in a person, 12 coins scattered into different directions when thrown into one direction indicate a couple's quarrel, and a coin sticking to one's palm indicates anger in the spirit of an ancestor.

These many different kinds of *chŏm* indicate only the materials that are used; there are also two different principles that are employed in the process of *chŏm*. The first is intuition by which the *chŏmjaengi* describes directly the ancestor or spirit who has caused the disease. This is used by the most supernaturally-gifted, and is based on magic and the depersonalization of the *mudang* who enters a trance or a state of ecstasy. Let me introduce this type of *chŏm* with the case of Chun Nya-kim. According to her, if a *chŏmjaengi* falls asleep during *chŏm*, an ancestor who has died of a narcotic is responsible; if she smells fish, it indicates one who had met a bloody death; if she suffers from abdominal pain, it means one who died during childbirth; if she is thirsty, it means one who was hanged or committed suicide by hanging; if her shoulder aches, it means one who has died in prison unjustly. She said that she could differentiate these senses during the *chŏm*.

The second method of *chŏm* is by questioning the inquirer. This method is practised in most fortune-telling cases. The following is an example of this kind:

C: (Client): Please look into this matter.

M: (*Mudang*): (ringing the bell and chanting incantation . . .) Something terrible has happened to your family.

C: Yes, something has happened, and I'm very worried.

M: There is an illness in your family.

C: Yes, someone is sick.

M: That's it, I told you, that's it!

C: You're incredible! My daughter-in-law is sick.

M: That's right. The spirit of Grandfather is telling me that your daughter-in-law is in bed with sickness (After more chanting, throws coins). It must have been since a month, or two, or three months ago. (At this time, the *mudang* after saying "a month", glances at the client and then says "two months" and glances one more time, and finally says "three months" as the face of the client beams brightly.)

C: You're right. It started three months ago. You're very good.

M: The spirit of Grandfather never lies. (At this time, rings the

bell again.) . . . One of your ancestors, there is one of your
ancestors who . . . who died unjustly, isn't there?

C: I really don't know . . .

M: Think carefully, there must have been someone.

C: (After a few minutes of pondering), Yeah, my uncle was
killed by a bomb during the Korean War.

M: That's it. That ancestor, your uncle is upset. His spirit is
upset. Because you have not treated him well, he is angry.
You must have forgotten to honor him with commemora-
tion services. That's why there is sickness in your family.

C: That uncle was killed right after he left the house quarreling
with me. (After a while, the client begins to shed a few
tears.) "What shall I do?"

M: You will have to honor him well. We can perform a *kut*.

In this example, we can find another principle of fortune-telling.
First, a question or statement that may be interpreted or understood
widely or imprecisely, is thrown to a client who, in a state of
susceptibility to hypnotic suggestion, provides voluntary responses
which reflect his or her state of mind and situation. The shaman, using
the responses, proceeds to elaborate on the diagnosis using the same
method.

What is important here is the trust of a client in the shaman and
his or her psychological readiness (*Bereitschaft*), or, susceptibility to
hypnotic suggestion. In some cases, if the client keeps silent, the
shaman becomes agitated.

The diagnosis of the sickness is obtained as a result of the *chŏm*,
and this seems directly related to the concept of disorders found in
early Korean society which diagnosed the following four causes of
sickness: a malevolent spirit, violation of a taboo, soul-loss, or curse. In
the first case, a wandering spirit, the spirit of an ancestor, any dead
person, or any evil spirit, is believed to have entered the body of the
patient and this possession is expressed in such terms as "controlled
by," "entered by," or "stamped by" evil spirits. This is equivalent to
Clements' "spirit intrusion" of the disease concept held in many

primitive societies, and accounts for the largest percentage as the perceived cause for mental disorders along with other chronic diseases in Korea.

Second, "violation of taboo" is pointed out as a cause for illness. This is equivalent to Clements' "violation of taboo" concept and, according to statistics, accounts for the next largest percentage as a perceived cause for mental illness. Although there is no accurate study to substantiate this, "violation of taboo" is believed to be a primary cause for general illness among shamanistic circles. There are several types in this category. The first is "violation of taboo" in the strictest sense. Incest, and the violation of a pregnant woman are examples, but these do not occur frequently. Another type is that of the "angry spirit", an expression also employed to refer to the case of "taboo." Here the emphasis is on the ill-treatment or neglect of a spirit who, in revenge, causes sickness. Other things, such as the inauspicious positioning of furniture, houses, trees, ill-chosen dates for house-repair, moving, weddings, travelling, etc., can also make the spirit of an ancestor angry. These also may be defined in a broader sense as "violation of taboo."

The third is "soul-loss." Although 9.7% of Koreans in rural areas attributed mental illness to "soul-loss", it is rare that an illness is diagnosed as "soul-loss" by shamans today. In Korea, expressions such as "lost spirit," or "drained of soul" are used.

Fourth, the concept of "curse" exists although it is seen only rarely. This is equivalent to Clement's "disease sorcery," but Lee has found it to be very rare in shamanistic circles in Korea. However, according to Yi Hŭng-hwa's *History of Chosŏn Exorcism*, during the Koryŏ Period, ceremonies of laying a curse were so abundant that the government decreed a ban on them, and although curses were not uncommon during the Yi dynasty, they have been extremely rare in this century. The existing practice of imprecation, however, can usually be found in the following examples. According to shaman Kim Chun-nya, when a wife is anxious to get rid of her husband's mistress, a ceremony of wishing sickness or evil on her is performed. According to another shaman called Yi, after a house is broken into by a thief, one pokes out the eyes of a catfish with a needle and buries it so that the thief becomes blind. Professor Chin Sŏnggi's research has also shown that the *Pangshwi* of Cheju Island is another form of cursing, although it is not practised in modern times, according to the observations of this author. The following sorcery was performed to get rid of a tyrannical mayor in a village. A wooden doll was carved in the form of a human being and put in a hedge. It was beaten by the village people on the first and fifteenth of every month, and the mayor became sick and died within a year. Because there are several examples of this kind, it seems hasty to conclude that a curse or "evil eye" does not exist in Korea, but we can say that the extent and frequency of this practice is now very limited and rare.

"Object-intrusion" as a cause for illness also exists but is very rare. It refers to the intake of spoiled meat, unclean water, or unclean food as the cause of illness. Although this is a case of material objects such as water and food, terms such as "unclean," and "spoiled" embrace the meaning of *sal-i kkyŏt-ta* (intrusion by an evil spirit), and thus extends its meaning to that of "spirit intrusion."

Once the diagnosis is completed within the range of the above causes, the method of treatment is chosen. The method can be any of the following four kinds of healing ceremony according to the severity of the illness, the nature of its cause, and the financial position of the patient: *Sonbibim* (simple praying), *p'udakkŏri, salp'uri,* and *kut* (grand healing ceremony). The fortune-telling is completed after the instruction about the chosen ceremony and its date has been chosen. Sometimes the date of the ceremony is set by a *sajujaengi* (another kind of fortune-teller).

Fortune-telling costs approximately 200-300 *wŏn* in the Seoul area and may be as little as 100 *wŏn,* or as much as 500 *wŏn,* according to circumstances. It takes place in either the home of the *mudang* or the *chŏmjaengi.*

Sonbibim (simple praying). Sonbibim is chosen when the nature of the sickness is not too severe and the sufferer has few financial resources. The *mudang* prays to many spirits with pure water and rice placed in front of her, and prays for a swift recovery to each of the twelve gods whom she hosts. The content of prayer differs with the cause of sickness so that, for instance, she prays for the removal of an evil spirit or the appeasement of anger in the spirit of an ancestor. The spirit who is believed to have caused the illness receives much more attention, as well as rice, and water, than do the others. Sometimes one prays to the evil spirit to depart once the food is offered. The *mudang* thus gives hope and assurance to the patient and the family by giving an approximate date of recovery. *Sonbibim* is usually performed under a divine tree, in a courtyard, at a mountain, or at the house of the patient or *mudang;* anywhere convenient to perform the ceremony.

The cost of *sonbibim* is not consistent but usually is around 5000 to 15,000 *wŏn.*

P'udakkŏri. This ceremony is generally performed for healing purposes. It is chosen when the cause of sickness is not severe and the financial situation is not such as to have an elaborate *kut.* According to Akiba and Akamatsu, the *p'udakkŏri* consists of four stages: *pujŏng, kamang, sangsan,* and *huhae.* Variation and flexibility seem to be allowed in the procedure depending on the *mudang* and the nature of the sickness. Since a detailed study of this procedure itself is not the purpose of this paper, it will be omitted, and the main components of *p'udakkŏri* in terms of treatment will be discussed.

The *mudang* prays to twelve gods in succession with food placed in front of her. During the prayer some *mudang* give divine messages (*kŏngsu*), a term which will be explained further when discussing *kut.* The particular god related to the sickness is given special attention, and lastly, the *mudang* prays even to the "evil spirit." After this, the patient's name, time and date of birth, and the phrase *"Taesu tae myŏng"* ("replace one's life and fortune") are written on a white sheet of paper, and placed in the wings of a rooster. If the patient is male, a cock is used and if female, a hen is used. Sometimes the rooster is clothed, and sometimes an egg, a puppy, or a pig is used in place of the rooster.

The *mudang* then chants supplications as she scratches a wicker trunk and strikes a gong. Some *mudang* imitate the act of twisting the neck of the rooster to death, or sometimes they actually kill it by strangulation. The rooster is then placed in an open shed and a wicker basket is placed over it. The patient or the family must not see this rooster as they leave the house. It is believed in shamanistic circles that the rooster used in such ceremonies either dies soon or no longer grows. *P'udakkŏri* can be performed at the patient's house but usually is done at the house of the *mudang* and should be attended by the patient himself, but if the illness is grave, only the patient's family will attend. This ceremony costs around 10,000-20,000 *wŏn*. As *p'udakkŏri* is defined by Kim as "healing by a rooster", it implies a connection to the "scapegoat" concept found in other primitive societies. It is thought that the disease and death of a human being is taken over by the rooster, and the process can be explained as a strong suggestion that the sickness will be cured.

Salp'uri. This healing ceremony is performed in cases of acute diseases. This kind of disease is believed to have been caused by intrusion of evil spirits (*sal-i kkyŏt-da*). The *mudang* prays to the gods in front of a table where corn-cake, corn, rice, ricecake coated with mashed red-beans, and fruits are placed. A cloth is put on the patient and taken off, and wrapped around the long sword with which the *mudang* dances. During the dance, the shaman imitates the act of driving out or striking the evil spirit, and the cloth is later worn by the shaman and then burnt.

The cost of *salp'uri* today is about 5000-15,000 *wŏn* in the Seoul area. From the perspective of psychotherapy, this ceremony indicates a suggestion for healing by reconciliation with the hostile object.

Pyŏng Kut. (Grand healing ceremony). This is performed when the sickness is severe and the cause considered serious. Of course, the financial burden which a patient can bear is also taken into consideration. The *pyŏng-kut* is not particularly different from other *kut* except that during its procedure *p'udakkŏri, salp'uri,* and *hwajŏn* are also included occasionally. When a particular ancestor is in the question "*kil-kkala chu-gi*" or preparation of the road)" is followed by "*chosang-gŏri*" (or a seance for ancestors). The *kut* is started with purification, and performed through twelve seances involving twelve gods. It used to be performed from early in the evening until the morning of the next day, but due to neighbor's complaints of sleep disturbance, it is customary today to perform between dawn and late evening. Sometimes it continues for two or three days.

The atmosphere of the *kut* differs according to the characteristics of each god in each *"gŏri"* (seance). For example, the *chaesok-gŏri* in which performers wear Buddhistic monk garb is accompanied by subdued and gentle music and dance, whereas the *changgun (general) gŏri* is performed with powerful and militant dance and songs.

Each *gŏri* is composed of three parts: *"yŏng-sin* (calling the god)", *"o-sin* (amusing the god)", and *"song-sin* (sending the god)". The *Yŏng-sin* starts with slow and gentle music and dance, and gradually changes into a violent dance as the tempo of music becomes faster and stronger. A song of exorcism is chanted during the first stage of the dance. During the time of this simple and repetitious dance, the *mudang* is expected to fall into a state of "trance," which is sometimes faked. In any case, the *yŏng-sin* is a calling ceremony, using the dance to induce the spirit to come, and a preceding stage of trance and "possession". All this is described by such terms as "covered with the god", or "possessed by the god" in shamanistic circles. The second part, *"o-sin"*, requires the presupposition that the *mudang* has entered the state of "possession". In other words, the *mudang,* during this stage, becomes "god" and her words are those of "god". She plays the role of the main god, adopting certain identifying characteristics. Sometimes she exchanges greetings with the patient, family, and the spectators, and plays comical games or issues stern warnings and punishments. During this time there is a divine message called *"kŏngsu"*. The *kŏngsu* in the case of the *pyŏng-kut* explains the cause of illness and suggests a way of healing it. This is equivalent to diagnosis and treatment. Then it tells when the sickness will be over. This is equivalent to prognosis and has the function of suggestion. During the ceremony several kinds of divination take place, using rice, flags or bamboo pipe. If an evil spirit or a wandering spirit is found to be a cause of illness, the *"changgun-gŏri"* is especially emphasized for the healing. During this time, the *changgun* god dances powerfully, and circles around the patient and drives out the evil spirit by imitating the act of striking out and stabbing. This is also indicative of "forecasting healing."

The third part, *"song-sin"*, is the procedure for sending away the god by placating it. The god departs as the fast and powerful dance gradually recedes into a slow and quiet dance, and this signals the removal of the spirit from the body of the *mudang.*

A variation which sometimes occurs is a rite called *chae-ung.* In it, a human-like doll is made out of straw and placed underneath the clothes of the patient. The doll is clothed with some article of the patient's clothing with the name and birth date of the patient inscribed on it. When it is thought that the spirit has descended into the shaman, she sings a *muga* (chant) as she imitates the act of sending away the evil spirit with a sword. After this, the straw doll is burnt or thrown away. "Chae-ung" is a disguised form of the word *"Ch'ŏyong"* which has been regarded as a powerful legendary god controlling serious infectious diseases and is assigned the role of scapegoat. In other words, the disease of the patient is believed to be taken over by *"chae-ung."*

Another variation is a rite called *"hwa-jŏn"* or fire-ritual. It is performed after sunset, and takes place just before the end of the *pyŏng-kut.* A straw bag is spread out in the yard, and a bed-sheet of the patient is placed in hot water and is used to wrap the body of the patient, to suggest a shroud on a corpse. The patient is placed on the straw bag and a dance which enacts the chasing away of the evil spirit is performed simultaneously with a fire- dance. At the end of a long stick, an oil-soaked rag is wrapped and ignited. With two sticks of this kind, a violent dance takes place. Since the evil spirit is believed to be fearful of fire, the fire is used to drive away the evil spirit. During the dance, rice-bran fried in oil is dropped into the fire to induce a larger flame. The shaman dances around the patient, shaking the fire-stick, and as the heat dries the wet bed-sheet, the patient begins to feel the heat. After 20 minutes of this, the patient is brought into a room on a stretcher, while the shaman then chases away the evil spirit in every corner of the house with the fire-stick. This *hwa-jŏn* has three different meanings. The first is a suggestion that all the evil spirits have been exorcised; the second, suggests the motif of death and rebirth; and the third is meant to dissolve guilt by simulation of the patient's death.

There are two other variations to note. The first is called *mugam* and is a sort of group therapy. It is usually performed in the afternoon when the participants are in an excitable state. The spectators dance with the shaman either alone or in a group, performing a dance which becomes faster and faster. During the dance, the spectator-participants fall into a state of trance by repetition of simple rhythms and movements. Some people experience a confusion of consciousness or hysterical convulsion, and often pour out their problems without restraint. Some women weep while dancing, and the whole process has the effect of group catharsis.

The second "*kil-kkala chu-gi* (preparation of the road)" is performed right after the "*chosang gŏri* (seance for ancestors)" in the *pyŏng-kut;* or in other *kut* when a particular ancestor is believed to be a cause of sickness. A long strip of fabric, about 5 meters long, dyed in yellow, ie prepared. The strip is held at each end by the *mudang's* helpers and the *mudang,* while dancing, jumps from one end to the other, stripping the fabric into two lengthwise pieces. This has the symbolic meaning of preparing the way for an ancestor as one sends away the spirit.

IV. Psychotherapeutic Significance of Shamanistic Treatment

Healing ceremonies, however primitive and incantational, are known to have psychotherapeutic effects. Successful mangagment of psychotic illness with shamanistic rituals is a well-known world-wide phenomenon, and much research on this has been done in Korea.

The most important function of this kind of ritual is cure, and while there is an inevitable element of superstition in it, my personal experience suggests that it has the possibility of treating psychogenic diseases such as psychoneurosis, psychosomatic disease, and schizophrenia, and has some effectiveness in comforting the patient and the family in the case of physical diseases. Not every psychogenic disease is cured, however, and in some cases, like that of schizophrenia, it can be dangerous. However, for the patient who has deep faith in sorcery, particularly in the case of anxiety-neurosis, hysteria, and psychosomatic disorders, sorcery has a clear effectiveness in its treatment. From a psychotherapeutic point of view, certain mechanisms of *kut* contribute to this effectiveness. What are these mechanisms?

Prognostication is the most frequently used and most basic healing method. Most shamanistic manipulation in kut and fortune-telling is based upon it. The effectiveness of prognostication is evident in *kŏngsu* (divine message), fortune-telling, purification rites, and *salp'uri* in the *kut*. They explain the cause of the illness, and based on that, manipulate the ceremony by entertaining or chasing away the spirit, thus assuring the patient that the illness will be over soon since the cause is removed. This forecast is not only effective in healing psychotic patients by giving assurance of cure but also in comforting the patient and family of the physiologically diseased.

Catharsis. The mechanisms of catharsis can be found at several stages of the *kut*. During the *kŏngsu* the patient or family members who receive the "message" often break down in tears and pour out problems and troubles. The *mudang* sympathizes with them and shares their sufferings. Women, while dancing *mugam,* often fall into trances as they release their frustrations through violent and powerful dance. During the *chosang* (a seance for the ancestor), people weep as they let out the suffering to their ancestors. During the *taegam-gŏri* (a seance for high government officers), it frequently happens that through overt sexual gestures, long-suppressed sexual desires and frustrations are released. Sometimes the shaman blatantly ridicules a particular class of people who are perceived to be an object of enmity by the spectators. This releases the ill-feelings of the people and their frustrations and suffering are transferred to the evil spirit in an enactment of killing the spirit. This also has the effect of catharsis.

Abreaction. The mechanism of typical abreaction can be found in the *chosang-gŏri* (ancestor seance) of the *kut*. People often have mixed feelings of respect and fear toward their ancestors and by confronting the ancestor directly the fear is dissolved. During this *chosang-gŏri* the shaman plays the role of an ancestor and either blames the descendants for their mistreatment, or promises to bless them in the future. At the time of departure, many embraces take place, expressing the sorrow of parting. At this time, the spectators reexamine their attitudes as they confront their own feelings toward their ancestors. Not only in *chosang-gŏri* but in all the seances, the direct confrontation with spirits which have been the object of fear accomplishes the effect of releasing the fear.

Persuasion. A *kut* has many parts in which persuasion takes place, from honoring ancestors to practical and educational virtues such as respecting one's parents and establishing a harmonious family, and adjusting in society. On January 23, 1972, the following observation was made in the *pyŏŏng-kut* of a schizophrenic patient at Seoul. The shaman tells the following *kongsu* (words of the gods) to the patient. "The disharmony in your family is the cause of disease. . . . There will be no diseases and the family will be peaceful when the parents love and understand the children and children treat their parents well. . . . If you would like to be cured, the parents should love the children more, and the children must listen to their parents." After the deathly atmosphere of *hwajŏn* (fire dance) stage, the shaman told the patient: "You've seen the fire. If you don't wake up from that delusion, you will be burnt to death by that fire. So, wake up!" This kind of "message" awakens awareness of one's surroundings, develops adaptability, and educates a person about life.

Transference. The phenomenon of transference becomes the core of shamanistic treatment, but treatment is impossible if the patient lacks confidence and faith in the *kut.* This faith implies that one identifies both *mudang* and gods with parents. The treatment of one's illness is possible when the words of the *mudang* are believed to be those of a god. Without the phenomenon of transference occurring in the process of *kut,* there is no effect.

Group Therapy. The healing ceremony, particularly kut, is performed to heal the patient, but is not concerned with the patient alone. It involves the family, the neighbors, and the spectators, because an unfortunate happening and its consequence are not limited to that individual alone. This idea is closely related to the traditional Confucian view of life which suggests that an individual finds his value chiefly in his relationship to the family and to the community. Accordingly, a *kut,* although performed chiefly for the benefit of one person, involves the whole group in its procedure and its effect.

The mechanisms for group therapy in *kut* can be found in several ways. First, a process of identification takes place during several seances of the *kut.* The spectators, for instance, share the happiness and sadness of the person involved as they feel identification with the one who receives the spirit-message. As the shaman is elevated to god-like status and falls into a state of trance, the spectators feel that they too are separated from their complexes and become god-like. They also feel like one family as they share the same good, joy, and sadness.

At this point, an identification through group identity takes place. Catalysis also occurs; the suffering of one person causes the surfacing of the hidden problems of the other, and this provides a chance for dissolving the problem together. Also, there is the effect of the universalization of one's problems. One realizes during the *kut* that others have the same problems, and thus universalizes his or her own problem, so that the procedure of solving the problems of another person becomes a way of solving one's own dilemma. In the *kut,* an atmosphere conducive to identifying oneself with others is created and this is the wisdom of group therapy.

These mechanisms do not act independently. Rather they interact, and a combination of mechanisms in condensed form, are used in a *kut.*

V. The Symbolic Meaning of Trance and Possession

Shamanistic treatment employs not one mechanism but a combination of mechanisms. The mechanisms such as catharsis, prognostication, transference, and abreaction are involved but so are symbolic approaches that are closely related to the state of unconsciousness. Of course, the shaman and the patients are not aware of these symbolic meanings, and a variety of hopes and desires in the realm of unconsciousness are symbolically achieved in a *kut* in the realm of conscious-ness, as Sandner pointed out in the case of Navaho Indians.

The symbolic meaning in shamanistic treatment is the state of "trance" and "possession." There are several other mechanisms in Korean rituals, but of most importance, are the phenomena of trance and possession. Several years ago, there was a heated debate over the ecstasy of shamanism in the academic circle of shamanistic studies. In Kim's conclusive and comprehensive study, it is suggested that the existence or non-existence of ecstasy is no more than a phenomenon which results from the process of differentiation and transformation of shamanism, and it exists as the primary element either as a cause or as a technique of showmanship in all regions of the country.

During the *kut*, the phenomena of trance and possession occur. If it is not a true state of trance, the shaman counterfeits it. The invocation of spirit is a necessary condition of the kut and the shaman transforms herself into the supernatural spirit relevant to each seance. If this does not take place, it is believed that the shaman transforms herself into a god, so that receiving messages from a god is possible. Because of this, both the shaman and the patient see the trance or possession as a sign of recovery or blessing.

One might also mention that in Korean shamanistic circles the existing concept of possession has a double meaning. They express the phenomena of trance and possession as "invited by the spirit" or "covered by the spirit"; expressions which indicate the confusion in equating "possession" with the simpler "trance." In shamanistic circles the agreed definition of possession indicates the total transformation of the identity of a person. However, any change in consciousness, loss of consciousness, or hysteric convulsions; in other words, the state of trance, is understood in Korea to be a state of possession. This confusion must have been derived from a strong belief in the validity of possession. It is appropriate to state that in Korean shamanism there does exist, in the strictest sense, the state of genuine possession, as well as the state of trance which is believed to be the state of possession.

There are reports in most societies, of religious practitioners who enter a state of possession by the repetition of simple rhythms and gestures, and thus receive the power of healing. It is only recently, however, that the symbolic meaning of "possession", and its effectiveness in healing has been discussed. In discussing this, it is convenient to borrow the concept of "transient regression of the ego" propounded by Wittkower, Prince, and Kraus. The phenomenon of possession that they describe in the rites of primitive societies is a kind of regression, in which the ego is unable to overcome the agony of life, and forgets the problem, by regressing into childhood. The extreme example of this can be found in schizophrenia. However, these scholars point out that the effect of "possession" in primitive rituals is temporary and reversible, and occurs in the healthy mind, so that it differs from the regression that takes place in the case of schizophrenia.

Trance and possession which fall into the category of "transient regression of the ego" become effective in several functions. They serve first as an escape mechanism. Trance and possession involve the depersonalization of a person so that an ego faced with harsh reality enters another world—that of fantasy. In other words, an ego confronting reality loses its function and lives in fantasy, and may come to dominate the entire personality of the person. This escape is significant in that it is temporary. A continuous state of escape may result in mental disorder, but a temporary escape for a period of time with a certain return to reality, sustains the healthiness of the ego. In other words, regression with a continuing relationship with reality, renders the possibility of healing.

Secondly, trance and possession have the symbolic meaning of realizing one's desires and dreams. Entrance into the phenomenon of trance and possession not only signals a simple escape from reality but also carries the meaning of symbolically realizing one's wishes that could not have been fulfilled in reality. In shamanistic circles, the depersonalized state of trance or possession is described as the "intrusion of spirits". This implies the establishment of a special symbolic relationship with "god" or "a god". As in many primitive societies, the concept of "possession" implies a symbolic hierogamy with a god, and it has often been suggested that this constitutes a symbolic realization of incest fantasy, the release of frustrated sexual desires, the compensation for our inferiority complex by elevating oneself to the status of a god, and the overcoming of fear by depending on a god who is also the image of one's parents. This kind of symbolic realization of one's wishes has the effect of dissolving psychological frustrations.

Third, the trance and the state of possession both carry the motif of rebirth. Because one's past life has been filled with pain and frustration, by regressing into the state of childhood, one forgets one's ego and returns to a state of revived energy as one wakes up from the trance. This carries the symbolic meaning of rebirth and provides a source of energy in a life that often seems too difficult to bear.

In conclusion, trance and possession is a kind of regression phenomenon that occurs either artificially or automatically and may be related to the healing effect of hypnosis. The phenomenon of possession in *kut* can be seen as an adaptive cultural mechanism designed to solve personal conflicts and to release the frustration of each individual.

VI. Cases of Shamanistic Treatment

In order to study the psychodynamic aspects of shamanistic treatment, discussing the cases in which *kut* is performed to heal diseases is necessary and helpful. I have personally participated in and observed the following rituals, conducted interviews with the patients about their medical and personal history and diagnosis, and have done a follow-up for each case.

Case 1. Mrs. Kim, housewife, 41 years old. She had a *pyŏng-kut* performed at her house on April 8, 1971, because of psychoneurotic symptoms. She had moved into her present house about a month before the date of the *kut*. Because she sold her previous house to move to a bigger house, she owed 40,000 *wŏn* at the time of moving. She had originally counted on receiving the sum of 50,000 *wŏn* which she lent to someone who went into bankruptcy before she could collect the money for the payment of the house. She did not receive either principal or interest, nor could she cancel the contract. After many sleepless nights, she bought her present house, taking out a mortgage of 40,000 *wŏn*. She could not sleep for days before and after the move. When she finally fell asleep, she would have nightmares and wake up with terrible headaches. Her heartbeat became irregular and she felt as if a fire were burning in her stomach. This feeling became so oppressive that she felt as if her throat were being squeezed. She then went to several fortune-tellers. Every one of them said that the position of the house was the cause of her symptoms and several said that *"T'ŏ-jut tae-gam"* (the spirit of house) was displaying his displeasure. Therefore a *kut* honoring *"t'ŏ-jut tae-gam"* was suggested.

Mrs. Kim was born as the first of seven children of a small farmer in a rural area. Her father's alcoholism had led not only to the loss of the family land, but also to neglect of his family prior to his death in 1961. The mother, in contrast, was active and aggressive, but was unresponsive to her children, and she had died in 1967, after suffering a severe nervous breakdown. Mrs. Kim herself had graduated with average grades from elementary school, and had then quit school to take a job to help her family financially. She had married at the age of nineteen.

Her husband had found a job in Seoul four years after their marriage, and of her four children, two daughters have jobs in a factory, and one son is in the army while the other is in junior high-school. Her husband is a security guard at a government office, but because of his low salary, she supplemented the family income by opening a small general store. The relationship of the couple is harmonious except for occasional quarrels because of the husband's drinking. Her mother often used to see fortune-tellers and shamans when she was troubled or her children became ill, and Mrs. Kim remembers how once when she had high fever a *mudang* came into her house and performed a *kut*. She reflected that in her childhood surroundings, when her father was unattentive and her mother domineering, the only way of feeling her mother's love was probably through fortune-telling occasions and *kut*. Her personality was strongly inclined to be egotistical, and while she did not know how to help and care for others, at the same time she demanded unquestioning love and total understanding from the members of her family. She could not endure the smallest degree of frustration and went to see fortune-tellers or shamans every time she was frustrated with love, or when she encountered any other problem. She requested a *kut* almost every year, and spent almost her entire income on these rituals. This may have been a result of her mother's reliance on frequent *kut*.

She had mixed views on the causes of disease although she had a relatively scientific understanding of certain illnesses such as mental, physical, and infectious diseases. She had a strong tendency to somatize her emotional problems, so that she saw her anxiety manifestations such as palpitation, indigestion, or pressure on her chest, as somatic illness. She also thought that these were caused by an angry ancestor, and that they could be cured by a *kut*. She went frequently to modern hospitals, but unless she found full relief, would resort to a *mudang*.

Her *pyŏng-kut* was successful. Her condition had grown worse a week prior to the ceremony, but on the day it was performed she felt much better. She wept throughout the ceremony and also fell into a trance. Her consciousness became clouded during the *mugam* (group dance), and as she danced, her face reddened and her breathing became fast. Her pulse became strong and fast and she was half conscious; a state probably of hyperventilation. She recovered after about five minutes and seemed at peace.

The following day when I met with her, the neurotic symptoms were gone. She said "after a *kut* I feel so peaceful and secure . . . I have to have it once a year . . . My heart is weak, you know . . .". She did not, in fact, have any heart trouble, but perceived anxiety symptoms as heart trouble. I met her once again on April 15, 1972. She had recently started having the same symptoms again. She said she was worried that she did not have enough money to get ready for another *kut*.

Case 2. Mrs. Lee, 34 years old, housewife. Born in Kwangwando, Yŏng-wŏl.

Mrs. Lee has been treated for hysteria which developed about 5 years ago. I observed the *kut* which was performed at her house on September 5, 1969.

This time the hysterical symptoms reappeared after she found out that her husband had had a mistress for about two months. After a fight with him, she continuously suffered from loss of appetite, foreign body sensations in the throat, headache, insomnia, and accelerated heartbeat. She frequently had to lie down, and sustained herself with water only. She often fell into the state of wandering in the mountains and manifested hysterical states of consciousness during which she would lie down motionless. She would curse her husband and his family and lament her unfortunate state. Her words were incomprehensible to her family and they thought that she had lost her sanity and was thus murmuring "nonsense". The family tried herb medicine to no avail. Her mother went to see a shaman and was told that the spirit of her father had entered her body, and thus she needed *pyŏng-kut* to appease the angry spirit.

Mrs. Lee dreamt the following on the day of selecting the date for the *kut*. "I was lying down with sickness on the floor in my old house. Mother had cooked thin rice gruel but I could not eat it. I felt I would die if I ate it. I longed to see my father but he was nowhere to be found. Someone told me that he was coming. Excited, I got up to greet him, but it was a big cow which came through the gate instead of my father. I greeted the cow very gracefully, however. It jumped over my body three times and ran away."

It was later revealed during the interview that she felt good about the dream and felt assured that she would recover her health after this *kut*.

The following is her own interpretation of the dream. "The cow represents the male ancestor. Seeing a cow in a dream is a good omen. The cow in my dream was my father. I always longed for my gentle father, and the appearance of the cow means that he would help me through."

Mrs. Lee was the fourth daughter of a countryside grammar-school principal. He had lived the life of a true educator, uncompromising and strong. He was a gentle and understanding father to his children. He died of a cerebral haemorrhage when she was nine years old. Her mother was an introvert, not expressive of her feelings. She was also businesslike and cold to her children. The couples' relationship was peaceful, patterned after the traditional male-dominant relationship in which proper courtesy rather than love was emphasized and practised. Mrs. Lee was an unwanted child since she was born when her parents expected a son after three daughters. Her mother, after giving birth to her, could not face the parents of her husband who urged their son to get a mistress in order to produce a male offspring. Because of his social and cultural status as a principal, he could not bring himself to do that. Mrs. Lee thus grew up in coldness, as an object of resentment from her mother. Mrs. Lee's own resentment toward her mother took a form of admiration for her father who had, in fact, treated her warmly. Her mother had two sons after she was born, and her grandparents'and parents' attention was naturally focused on her brothers, and she felt more isolated and lonely. She was a model student at home and at school. When her father died suddenly when she was nine years old, she wept bitterly. His death was too painful for her to bear. It was her only joy to see her father at school and at home to sit on his lap.

In addition, after her father's death, she could not continue her education. Finishing elementary school, she helped with the housework until she was seventeen and she moved to Seoul to work at a factory. In her frustration at not being able to continue her education and facing hardship in her life, she lived in constant resentment and yearning for her father. At the age of twenty she went back home and married her present husband who was a pupil of her father. He graduated from the local teachers' college and taught in elementary school. They moved to Seoul five years later and opened up a button wholesale shop. The business was good and life secure. She has one son and three daughters. She was near frigidity in her sex-life, and after sex, she always suffered from headaches and backaches. Unable to release her frustrations, she stored up her anxieties and had lately become anxious that her husband might leave her for a better educated woman.

The first time she approached a shaman was five years ago when she developed the first symptoms of hysteria. As that time her husband's business was prospering and he moved up in status, becoming a wholesale merchant. She began to suspect that he was wasting money on some other women as he did not give her enough housekeeping money. She then started to see fortune-tellers, and *mudang,* in the company of neighborhood women.

Her views on diseases were mixed. She had previously had a modern outlook but gradually developed a shamanistic one after frequenting fortune-tellers and *mudang.* She would visit both specialists in herbal medicine and modern hospitals for the same disease and see a shaman at the same time.

Her *pyŏng-kut* was successful. During the *kut,* the *mudang* told her that her illness was caused by the spirit of her father who was displaying his displeasure at not being treated properly. Consequently, the *kut* was concentrated on the *chosang-gŏri* (ancestor seance) and she cried, thinking of her father during this ceremony. Feeling that her life would have been better if he were alive, she poured out all her hardships while the *mudang* played a role of her father. The words of her father were those of warm consolation and blessing. He advised her to live harmoniously. She cried out loud at the last scene of the ceremony in which the spirit of her father was parting.

In fact, she had begun to feel better before the day of the *kut,* and reassured of her special relationship with her father through her dream the night before, she needed the *kut* to reaffirm it. She was a little tired but all her symptoms were gone completely at the end of the *kut.*

Two years after the *kut,* I interviewed Mrs. Lee again. She had had one more *kut* during that period, because her illness had reappeared and her son was suffering from arthritis. After the *kut,* she recovered and her son was treated at the hospital, since in the *kut,* the shaman had told her to "go to the east for medical treatment." She went to a hospital located in the east. "I am not fully recovered. Many things happened, and isn't it nervous anxiety? My father's spirit is so stubborn that it wouldn't leave my body." In this case the characteristic symptoms of hysteria, "secondary gain," "craving for sickness," and "incest-fantasy" can be found.

Case 3. Kim, sophomore in high school, 17 years old, male, born in Seoul.

He was hospitalized on December 7, 1971, in a mental hospital after being diagnosed as schizophrenic. Since the autumn of 1971 he had worn a serious look on his face and would not associate with others, often bursting out in anger, abusing his father. While hospitalized, he had a *pyŏng-kut* performed at the suggestion of his grandmother.

He was born the second son of a small farmer on the outskirts of Seoul. His father's inherited land became the site of a housing project and the price soared, so he sold his lands and became an overnight millionaire. The father had only a grammar school education and was meticulous, but was lacking in resoluteness and was inclined to nag. He was an only child. The patient's mother had died of stomach cancer in 1965 and he had been raised by a stepmother. The patient had two brothers and five sisters. Two of his sisters were married and three were younger. One brother stayed home after finishing high school. There are two step-brothers by his step-mother.

Kim from his childhood was always short-tempered. Overprotected by a family who regarded the male offspring more highly than the female, he lost his mother at the age of ten. Since then, his grades had fallen and he became melancholy and silent. From age fourteen, he began to have an inferiority complex thinking that he was too short for his age, although he was of average height. From then on, he thought his nose too small, his eyebrows too thin, his forehead too narrow, and came to believe that these deficiencies caused everything to go wrong. He started to develop fears that other people would talk behind his back and regard him with contempt. These symptoms became so severe that outsiders began to notice it.

Kim's view of illness was a scientific one and he did not have any shamanistic conceptions. Once a year his family had a *kut,* and he regarded it with shame and resentment. He did not know what kind of treatment was good for him since he was suffering from schizophrenia, and his skepticism meant that neither he nor his family nor the shaman expected a cure to result from the performance of a *kut.*

The causes of the illness discovered during *kut* in the form of a *kŏngsu* (message) was that an ancestor spirit was angry about his maltreatment and that the family lacked harmony and love.

"In a family like this, how can you expect your son to be healthy? Since everyone is demanding that his own interests be served and is disregarding the others, how can the family be peaceful and harmonious? That's why I (the ancestor spirit) gave you this punishment. "Please be harmonious and work hard, and please be obedient and get medical care. Do your best in taking care of yourself. You will be cured around the second month of the lunar calendar". This was the consoling message of the ancestor.

Those who benefitted most from this *kut* were the patient's grandmother, step-mother, and three of his aunts. They all expressed relief and received consolation. The patient himself said "I don't feel anything. It's the same as usual." However, in the second lunar month, which the shaman had designated as the time for recovery, the patient was completely cured of his illness, and discharged from the hospital.

In this case, the *kut* did not cure the illness, but rather helped the medical treatment to be successful.

Case 4. Mrs. Chung, 26 years old. Housewife, born in Seoul.

Mrs. Chung had a *kut* performed on September 5, 1970, but her illness became worse. She had had an arranged marriage two years earlier, and immediately started to develop conditions such as insomnia, loss of appetite, headaches, and the delusion that her mother-in-law was stealing her possessions. She watched every movement of her mother-in-law, and often fought with her, claiming that everyone was conspiring to make a fool out of her. She wandered in the middle of the night without going to sleep.

She was the first daughter of five children in a farm family. Her father had relatively large landholdings, and he was gentle, generous, and warm toward his children. Her mother, in contrast, was hysterical and unreceptive. The patient had received a junior-high school education, and by the time she reached adolescence, she had developed a strong resentment toward women in general, and this made the relationship with her mother particularly trying. At age fifteen her mother died of cerebral haemorrhage. This event was a great shock and she became melancholy as she felt both resentment and guilt toward her mother. She married at the age of nineteen, and after her marriage, a step-mother moved into her father's house. She was never on good terms with her step-mother, and disliked her presence.

Her husband is an elementary school teacher and a good person, very tender and cheerful. He cared for her deeply, but she complained that he was trying to get away from her. She did not have a good relationship with her mother-in-law.

She was obstinate, stubborn, and distrustful of others. She had scientific views about illness and rejected shamanistic views, but was knowledgeable from childhood experiences about shamanism. Her mother, when not feeling well, had always had *kut* performed and *kut* reminded her of her mother.

The decision to have a *kut* was not entirely her own. Her mother-in-law went to see a shaman and made arrangements and when her illness was diagnosed, the shaman suggested it was caused by the anger of her mother's soul which was bent on revenge, and thus required a *chinogwi-kut* (a requiem) to appease the spirit.

During the *kut,* she underwant many emotional changes and became violent. She abused the *mudang* and the surrounding women and prayed for forgiveness to her mother. During the *mugam* (dance) stage, she fell into a state of possession and shouted, "I am your grandfather. I will make you prosperous. Why is this family in disharmony? Give devotion to me every morning." Later she could not remember what she had said, and the *mudang* interpreted her words to be those of her mother's spirit. Even after the *kut* was over, her excited and disorganized behaviour continued. After that she fell into the state of possession intermittently and reenacted the gestures of her mother and grandfather. Eight days later, at my suggestion, she was hospitalized at the mental hospital in which I was working. After a month's treatment, she fully recovered and was discharged.

In conclusion, there are cases in which the *pyŏng-kut* actually can alleviate symptoms, but this effect was limited to psychotic diseases and to those patients who had faith that he or she would be cured by a *kut.* In other cases of psychogenic illness, if the patient did not have faith in the *kut,* and in the case of organic diseases, the effectiveness of the *kut* extended to that of group therapy that relieved the fear and anxiety of the family members rather than the patient himself. It is also to be remembered that even if the *kut* seems successful in curing the illness, it is only temporary and the symptoms are likely to recur.

VII. Cultural and Psychiatric Problems of Shamanistic Treatment

The methods of shamanistic treatment and its psychotherapeutic effects have now been discussed and I would like to turn now to the possible influence of this particular method on the personality or behaviour patterns of the Korean people.

The first problematic issue in *kut* is its "projective" aspect, which is a basic element of the shamanistic perception. In this projection, the problems of an individual are passed to a supernatural being, thus hindering the recognizing of the problem as one's own. Rather than accepting and confronting problems as one's own, by projecting them onto supernatural beings, many persons find it easier to seek shamanistic treatment. As shown in our case studies, the conflicts caused in the ego are believed to have been caused usually by ancestor spirits and consequently, honoring the ancestors is believed to be the way to solve the problems.

The projective treatment which is the basic element of the *kut* not only in Korea but also in other countries, raises the following problematic points:

1) The lack of "insight". Murphy, in studying shamanism on the Island of St. Lawrence, pointed out that this form of treatment was lacking in "insight" and many other people agree with his argument. In fact, it is hard to find in Korean shamanism, the "insightful approach" that is frequently mentioned in Western psychotherapy. Shamanistic ceremonial seems to be lacking the insightful approach that makes the patient aware of the cause of the illness, and instead simply attributes it to a supernatural cause. However, this is not to say that shamanist treatment in Korea is entirely without insight. At several stages of the *kut,* one can find elements which promote insight about human relationships, such as those between the patient and his ancestors, family, and neighbors. Therefore, in Korean shamanism, the insightful approach of Western psychotherapy which looks into the

core of the problem is absent, but instruction in human relationships is abundant.

2) Projective treatment and the paranoid tendency. The relevant mechanism which promotes paranoid tendency is projection. Shamanism is inclined to be projective and is rich in paranoid personalities. It is generally accepted that projective shamanistic society is a paranoid-prone society. Repeated projective treatment clouds one's perception and ability to identify the problems as one's own and induces the development of a paranoid personality, and sometimes of paranoid schizophrenia, a fact which has been found to be true in the studies of Wittkower and Kennedy. The effectiveness of the projective treatment, although it is easily achieved, is therefore problematic.

3) Temporary "cure" and high rate of recurrence. This is evident in the fact that of the seventeen cases I studied, five resulted in a recovery which lasted only a short time and the patients in all five cases requested another *kut* within a year or two. Shamanistic treatment is not causative, but projective, so that the real source of the problem is not confronted. The popularity of shamanistic treatment probably says a great deal about the Korean mentality.

A final point I might make about shamanistic treatment is its strong humanistic element. Although supernatural beings are identified as the sources of illness in a *kut,* it is to be remembered that the shaman focuses mainly on the welfare of human beings and manipulates the spirits. The focus is therefore this-worldly. The "gods" of shamanism are not omnipotent, nor do they differ much from human beings. The curses that are so familiar in the West are virtually nonexistent in Korean shamanism, and likewise, shamanistic rituals do not create enemies. The spirits who cause suffering to people are appeased and honored during the *kut* and they become friends to the people. The emphasis of the *kut* is not simply the suffering of an individual alone, but is extended to that of the family and neighbors. If the *mudang* asks the patient to describe other wishes during the *kut,* the response is likely to be "harmony and peace" in the family and in the village. The agony of one individual is therefore that of the family and society, and the suffering of the family and the neighbors is also that of the individual. The individual does not exist alone, but in relation to others.

This humanistic aspect of shamanistic treatment is influenced by Korean humanistic culture which has existed from ancient times. The Korean philosophy of life which values cooperation and inter-dependency more highly than competition and individualism is closely related to the humanistic elements of shamanistic treatment. A thorough study of this relationship should be undertaken in the near future.

VIII. Conclusion

My four-year study of shamanistic rituals or *kut* has revealed to a certain extent the complexities of the ritual. The mechanisms of the *kut* include such things as auto-suggestion, forecasting, catharsis, abreaction, persuasion, transference and group therapy. These mechanisms, coupled with the symbolic meanings that appear in the *kut* contribute to the relieving of the anxiety of the patient, and it is clear that therapeutically, the *kut* is effective for some psychogenic illness such as anxiety-neurosis, and for the patient who has a deep faith in the shamanistic view of the cause of illness. However, in the cases of organic disorders the effectiveness of the *kut* is most evident as a form of group therapy, relieving the anxieties both of the patient and his or her family, rather than as a cure for the disease itself.

Lastly, the principal nature of shamanistic treatment has been defined as "projective". The consequential problems that arise from this phenomenon have a close relationship with the psychology of the Korean people.

Her symptoms were caused by projecting her yearning for her father and her guilty feeling and hostility against her mother into shamanistic ritual, but the *kut* only aggravated her symptoms. She said that the spirit of her grandfather and her grandmother were fighting in order to win her over. The spirit of her gentle grandfather was the image of her father, while the spirit of her grandmother was that of her own mother. The conflicting feelings of her childhood burst out through the *kut* and aggravated her illness.

Case 5. Mrs. Yang, 30 years old, housewife, Seoul.

Mrs. Yang fell into an acute state of panic after quarreling with women in her neighborhood over a trifling matter on June 5, 1972. During the quarrel, the other women called her "bitch", "wanton", and "prostitute". This put her into a panic. She could not sleep nor eat and began to murmur incomprehensible words. As this lasted over a week, her mother-in-law went to see a shaman and was told that an ancestor spirit was angry and that a *pyŏng-kut* would have to be performed. She agreed.

The patient is the eldest of three children of a family which owns a general store. Her father was industrious and devoted to his family and her mother was cheerful, affectionate and equally devoted to her children. When she was thirteen, her father died of tuberculosis and her mother died of stomach cancer the following year. Left as an orphan, she did housework at her relatives' homes, while her siblings were put in an orphanage. She got a job at a textile factory at the age of eighteen and took her younger siblings out of the orphanage and began to live independently. The money earned from the factory was not enough for her new responsibilities, and she got a job at a tea-house. At the age of twenty-three, after working at the tea-house for four years, she married her present husband. He was a factory worker with a junior high school education.

Their marriage was a good one, but even though he was understanding and protective of her past, she became regretful of her dissolute past life and became preoccupied with worry that her three daughters would grow up and find out about her past. Meanwhile, a quarrel with the neighborhood women, in which her shameful past was brought out, put her into state of panic.

She struck me as quiet, docile and patient. She had relatively scientific views on disease, and did not have any inclination to shamanism. She said clearly after she was recovered that her mental breakdown was a result of psychological conflict over her past life.

The *kut* was not successful in her case. It only brought her dormant dilemma to the surface and aggravated her anxiety more. The violent and fearful dance of the shaman further increased her fear, and she shouted abuse at the shaman, identifying her with those neighborhood women with whom she had quarrelled. The underlying hostility toward those women was directed at the shaman.

The above five cases are representative of seventeen cases I have observed. Due to lack of space, the other twelve cases are omitted here and although seventeen is a small number in which to find any statistical meaning, it is helpful in describing general aspects of the shamanistic treatment.

Of the seventeen cases, five involved males, and twelve involved females. Two of them were under 10 years old, one in the teens, two in the twenties, seven in the thirties, four in the forties, and one in the fifties. As to educational level, seven graduated or dropped out of junior high school, and the rest either graduated from elementary school or received no formal education. The breakdown of medical diagnosis showed eight were schizophrenic, five had a tendency toward "possession," and two were suffering from psychoneurosis; so altogether fifteen tended toward psychological mental illness. There were five cases in which the patients suffered from physiological diseases such as epilepsy, herniation of intervertebral disc, pneumonia, nephritis, and hemiparesis. It is particularly interesting that regardless of the type of illness or the name of the spirit, the cause of illness in the most cases were attributed to the ancestor spirit. Using Clement's concept; there were eight cases caused by possession and nine by violation of taboo.

As for the effectiveness of the treatment, four patients of psychoneurosis and one patient of schizophrenia recovered temporarily and the rest either had their condition aggravated or were not affected by it at all. The factors that contribute to the effectiveness of treatment are diagnosis of the sickness, the patient's view of shamanistic treatment, and his confidence in such treatments. It is generally believed that psychoneuroses such as hysteria and anxiety-neurosis are easily cured by *kut* but in the case of schizophrenia, regardless of the patient's confidence level, it is likely to aggravate the illness. Of course, organic diseases will not be cured by healing ceremonies.

The patient's view of disease is another factor. It is interesting that a *kut* was effective in the cases of hysteria and anxiety-neurosis, although the patients regarded favorably both the concept of shamanistic healing and modern medical treatment. In the case of schizophrenia, although there was a high expectancy level among the patients, the *kut* aggravated the illness. I conclude from this that the *kut* stimulated the weak ego of the patient to such an extent that he could not cope with it.

Finally, faith in the *kut* is the basic element that influences its effectiveness. Out of the seventeen patients, four of them who were suffering from psychoneurosis had long been accustomed to shamanistic belief and its rituals, and felt assured of its effectiveness from their previous experiences. The *kut* was successful in these cases. Out of eight schizophrenic patients, only three held strictly modern views on disease and the rest had both a modern and shamanistic outlook; and none of them had clear expectations, because they did not know what kind of treatment was advisable as a cure.

Role Playing Through Trance Possession in Korean Shamanism

K orean shamans can be roughly divided into two types: possessed, or charismatic shamans, and hereditary shamans. The former, called *naerim mudang,* are typically found in the northern half of the Korean peninsula. After suffering from *sinbyŏng* [1] an illness which is generally interpreted as a sign of a shamanistic calling, a potential *naerim mudang* apprentices herself to an established shaman from whom she acquires the knowledge and skills aopropriate to her new occupation. The two women establish a "spirit mother"-"spirit daughter" relationship, with the spirit mother later conducting the initiation rite which transforms her apprentice into a full-fledged shaman. [2] In the course of their rites, these shamans not only become possessed and experience ecstatic trance states themselves but may also induce their clients to do the same.

The hereditary shamans, called *tan'gol mudang,* are found in the southern half of the Korean peninsula. They are recruited not through possession sickness but simply by being born into a shaman's family. Though this type of shaman does not undergo trance possession herself, she may cause other persons or even objects to become possessed in the course of a rite.

There are at least three different types of trance possession in Korean shamanism. The first, performed by the *naerim mudang,* can be seen in the rite performed to guide the spirit of a deceased person to the otherworld. In this type of rite known as a *chinogwi-kut,* the shaman plays the role of the deceased. She talks, cries, and otherwise communicates with the dead person's family. Details of the *chinogwi-kut* will be interpreted in the following paragraphs through a careful description of an actual *kut.*

This *chinogwi-kut* was held in mid-August, 1981, for Yun-jin Noh, an ordinary citizen who had lived the uncomplicated life of a small-town florist. A month before the kut, he had died of hypertension at the age of 62. In compliance with the wishes of his widow, an old shaman named Yŏng-ja Cho came to take charge of the entire ritual service. The shaman, aged 74, had been blind for ten years. Her reputation was well-known among the people of her province. Not only did she have several spirit daughters but she also had her own shaman altar in Yuyang-ri, Yangju-gun of Kyŏnggi-do where many *kut* had been performed.

When the day of the *kut* came and all the preparations for the rite had been completed, the shaman held the ritual with the help of her three spirit daughters, Kyŏng-ae Kim (aged 42), Yong-rae Park (45), and Suni Lee (57). The widow and younger sister of Mr. Noh, three daughters-in-law, and two wives of his nephews attended the shaman. It should be noted that all the participants were women, except for the eldest son of the deceased.

The *kut* was divided into a natural progression of 16 rites. The order of the first nine was as follows:

1. *Pujŏng-gŏri,* purifying the altar, the opening ceremony.
2. *Sangsan-gŏri,* prayer to the mountain god for protection.
3. *Pyŏlsang-gŏri,* prayer to the Spirit of Smallpox for expulsion of diseases.
4. *Obangsinjang-gŏri,* prayer to the Warrior Official and spirits of the Five Directions for protection.
5. *Sangsantaegam-gŏri,* prayer to the Low-Level Spirit-Official for protection.
6. *Ponhyang-gŏri,* prayer to the guardian spirits of the village for protection.
7. *Chosang-gŏri,* prayer to the spirits of ancestors for protection.
8. *Songju-gŏri,* prayer to the household god for happiness.
9. *Ch'angbu-gŏri,* prayer to the deity of dead actors for protection from accidents.

The opening nine rites, which are also basic to the Family Ritual for Happiness, were performed on the veranda of the house, in front of the altar erected there. The remaining seven rites, the main parts of the *chinogwi-kut* for the dead, were held in front of another altar erected for the dead man in the yard of the house.

One of the spirit daughters, Kyŏng-ae Kim, performed the following two seances (10-11): *arin-kamang-gŏri* (invocation of mournful gods) and *chungditaewang-gŏri* (prayer to the Ten Kings of the underworld for the repose of the departed soul). Then, the shaman, wearing a yellow robe and a hemp cloth tied around her head with a straw cord, came into the yard through the front gate. She had a stick in her right hand, a shaman's brass bells in her left hand, and a dried fish wrapped with white paper (symbolizing the abode of the departed spirit) on her back. She then began the 12th seance, the *saje-gŏri*.

The *sajch-gŏri* involves the acting out of a pocket melodrama between the family of the dead man and the shaman herself who becomes a greedy messenger from hell. The shaman says, "The deceased told me 'we are so rich that we can afford to give you a huge feast.' But what a poor treatment! Your goddamned dead husband made a fool of me." The messenger (the shaman), in a rage, comes to throw away the abode of the departed spirit (the dried fish on her back). Then the members of the family, apologizing for their lack of hospitality, give the messenger some money. (This also means that the family has asked the messenger not to take the deceased to hell.) After receiving the money, the messenger sings *"Saje t'aryŏng"* ("The Messenger's Song," sung by the shaman) while holding the dried fish in her left hand and shaking the brass bells with her right hand.

Here is an abstract of the *"Saje t'aryŏng"*: When the florist died of hypertension, the messenger came to take him to be judged. They journeyed to the gate of the otherworld, where the Ten Kings will give him judgement. The shaman (the messenger) asks these judges to allow the dead man to live on the lotus blossom peak in paradise, despite the fact that the dead man was not noted for his acts of charity. The shaman informs the Ten Kings that if the dead man ever lives on earth again he will be extremely kind, considerate, and charitable.

When the *saje-gŏri* ends, Yŏng-ja Cho, wearing a red robe and a large wig decorated with a crown, continues with the 13th rite. It is called *malmi-gŏri* (recitation of the myth of Princess Pari). In this seance, the invocation is addressed to the founding-spirit of the shamans, Pari-kongju (lit. "Rejected Princess"). This title refers to the guiding of the deceased's soul to the otherworld by Pari-kongju.

Pari-kongju, the seventh and last daughter of a king, was rejected by her parents who had wanted a prince to be born. She was abandoned and had to endure many hardships. When her parents fell sick and died, she obtained medicinal water from another world. With this she brought her parents back to life. Thereupon she herself became a deity, endowed with the gift to guide the deceased to the otherworld, and became the foundress-spirit of shamans.

The shaman recited *"Pari-kongju,"* a long shaman song of epic character, for more than an hour, shaking the brass bells in her left hand and beating a *changgo* (hourglass-shaped drum) with a *changgo* stick in her right hand. At several points during this performance, Pari-kongju does succeed in taking the dead to a better world. Also, the family shows their concern by wailing continuously throughout this part of the ceremony.

This seance contains two ideas which seem worthy of deeper consideration. First, after all her suffering, Pari-kongju is given an elixir, by which she brings her deceased parents back to life. This becomes the reason why, during this rite, she is asked to lead the soul of the deceased to a better world. Second, after her return in triumph, she chooses to renounce royal ways and becomes the benefactor of the despised shamans. She calls herself Inwi-wang ("King of the Despised"). This may symbolize a refusal to compromise with the male-first tradition of her society.

After the blind shaman finished reciting the long epic song, she allowed Yong-rae Park, her spirit daughter, to perform the 14th rite, *toryong-gŏri* (circumambulation) in her place. With a fan and a shaman's knife in her hand, the spirit daughter puts on a red robe and a large wig. Shaking her brass bells, the shaman proceeds to go around the dead man's altar three times. She moves erratically, going three steps forward and then two steps backward to the beat of shamanistic music. The members of the dead man's family follow the shaman, weeping. The widow carries a portrait of the deceased, and her two daughters-in-law hold a new robe for the dead, incense, and candles. This circling around the altar symbolizes the journey of the dead man from this world to the gates of the otherworld.

After this circling is completed, the shaman holds in one hand a fan which she opens and closes continuously above her head. In her other hand, she twists a knife in the air, twice to the left above her head, and then throws the knife to her assistant on the opposite side of the altar. The assistant catches the knife and returns it to the shaman again. This process symbolizes the purification of the area around the altar by the act of circling. Then the shaman dances a unique kind of dance, involving various hops, skips, and/or jumps. And then she sings a song for the dead. This song will hopefully guarantee the dead man's entrance into paradise. Next the shaman performs the 15th rite, *chungdi-garŭm-gŏri* (divided cloth bridge rite). This rite needs a *siwang-po* in order to be performed. The *siwang-po* is made of two different kinds of cloth, hemp and cotton, each of which is 7-feet long. Six cloth bridges are prepared for three people: the deceased, his mother, and his brother who had been killed in the Korean War (two bridges for each person). The moment four members lift one of the cloth bridges up over their heads, pulling its four edges, the shaman, beating the cymbal, goes under the bridge. After turning left and right two times, she proceeds through the cloth bridge *(siwango-po)* with her breast, thereby splitting each of the cloth bridges in half. This ceremonial action is considered to have opened the way to paradise for the dead by making smooth the road to the world beyond. There are also two other reasons why the cloth bridges are used. First, the hemp cloth, which is called "unclean bridge" or "*siwang* bridge", opens the way to the Ten Kings of Hell. Second, the cotton cloth, called the "clean bridge" or "Buddhist bridge," opens the way to Buddha or paradise. As the shaman marches through the cloth bridge, the family of the deceased hurriedly put down money on the split cloth. This act symbolizes their best wishes for the dead. [3]

In splitting the cloth, the shaman demonstrates an extreme state of emotion, in other words, a compressed, determined attempt to cut off the attachment between the living and the dead. In this way, the act of splitting the cloth not only opens the way to the world beyond for the dead, but it also splits the dead from the living.

The split *siwang-po* is then brought in and out of a thorny gate three times. This is a kind of prayer for the dead, expressing the hope that he will not be entrapped in the gate when entering the world beyond. When the *kut* ceremony ends, the *siwang-po,* along with the paper image of the spirit and the clothes of the dead, is set on fire before the front gate of the house. Next, before the invocation of the spirit seance the shamans and members of the family set up an offering table in front of the altar of the deceased; and they perform a memorial ceremony for the deceased, and the family of the deceased weep for him. As is not the case with the Confucian ceremony for the deceased in which only males are allowed to participate, both men and women participate in the *kut* ceremony.

Finally, a seance, the *nokch'ongbae-gŏri* (invocation of spirits) is performed. The shaman, wearing a paper image of a spirit on her head, invokes the spirit of the deceased by singing an invocation chant in time to shamanistic music; and while dancing wildly, the entranced shaman becomes possessed by the spirit of the deceased. At that moment, tinkling her bells, she begins to recite a mournful message from the deceased. In this way the shaman becomes the deceased and plays the part of the deceased. Shrieking with "Oh!, How awful!" or "Aaah! How awful!" she weeps over the death and falls into a faint. Supported and awakened by the family of the deceased, she (the deceased) grasps his wife, sympathizes with her by saying "What will become of you alone in the future?" and consoles the widow in her sorrow. At the same time the widow weeps bitterly, grasping the deceased. And then the mournful message continues as follows: "I haven't benefitted from my parents and tried hard to make a living, and so we had little leisure time." In response to the message, the widow irritably screams: "Don't you remember what I said? I said I wanted to die first. Why did you die first?" Again the message: "Well, a widow's better than a widower. You, whelp, what made you so hot-tempered?" "Oh! this is the last time you get hot-tempered." As if the deceased were living there takes place a quarrel between the couple. They are then parted, drink together, and smoking cigarettes, are reconciled with each other. Turning to the daughters-in-law, the deceased says, "Live your lives happily. You sisters-in-law, have affection for each other," and then turning to his wife again, "Please take good care of the housekeeping in my absence." Hearing the message, the family of the deceased embrace each other and weep.

Next the deceased claims his possessions (his watch, his hat, and clothes) but is irritated by the fact that the clothes are winter-clothes stuffed with cotton, and not summer-clothes. The deceased cries, "Where can I go on this sultry summer day with these cotton clothes on?" Then a comic skit with the clothes takes place. At last, he asks for a digestive aid for his stomach pain. His wife answers, "You've already died. Isn't that enough? Why do you, a dead person, want some medicine?" At the sight, the relatives ask the deceased to leave, saying "Why don't you stop complaining, rather than commenting on the diseases of your wife?" "Please give help to your son and daughters," and "Please stop grieving for your family and fly away without any lingering attachment." In response to that, the deceased says "I'll give you no more grief. Don't worry (about me), but take good care of your lives," and, "Now I'm leaving." The shaman again dances to the shamanistic music, and the *nokcho'ngbae-gŏri* is completed.

The major part of the *chinogwi-kut* has now been completed. Finally, the *kut* ends with a *twijŏn-gŏri* (feeding miscellaneous spirits and sending them away).

The above paragraphs have given a brief explanation of how one might deal with many dangerous spirits which haunt a family caught in a lingering attachment to the dead person. On the other hand, it has also been shown how the deceased can be made to join the ranks of helpful ancestral spirits through the processes of a shamanistic rite, the *chinogwi-kut*. These ancestral spirits will help and protect the family's posterity. And the family survivors, through participation in the dramatic process, come to believe in the deceased's entry into the blissful otherworld and are thereby relieved of bitter grief.

A second type of role playing involving trance possession is carried out by the hereditary shamans, or *tan'gol mudang*, along the eastern coast of southern Korea. In this case one of the family members of the deceased, usually a wife, mother, or sister, holding a spirit basket, is possessed by the deceased. The shaman addresses various statements or questions to the deceased, and the deceased (the possessed member of his family) responds without saying a word by causing the basket to shake if the particular statement is correct or if the answer to the question is affirmative. In the other case, however, the deceased expresses his sorrowful message in words. This shows that members of the dead man's family, who are laymen, possessed by the spirit, play the role of the *naerim mudang* type of shaman found in the northern half of Korea. Through this device, the living can communicate with the dead. We can demonstrate this kind of role playing with an example of *sumangogu-kut* (shaman ritual for drowned fishermen).

The shaman ritual was performed as a joint memorial service for eight young fishermen at a small fishing village of two hundred households and a population of about one thousand of Taebyŏn-ri, Kijang-myŏn, Yangsan-gun in Kyŏngsangnam-do, for two days from December 12th to 13th, 1981. The young fishermen were fishing for anchovies on a small (13-ton) fishing boat named Tae-hwan in the Kampo sea when they met a sudden gust of wind on the first day of November. Except for the captain who had rescued himself by swimming to shore, all of the crew were drowned. The villagers couldn't even find their corpses.

Accidents like this happen from time to time in the villages of Korea's east coast. About 100 fishermen still drown or disappear every year. Whenever an accident takes place, the villagers perform a *kut* for the deceased spirits. Especially on the east coast, we can see *kut* that portray the grief of women like those described in "Riders to the Sea," a drama written by J.M. Synge (1871-1909).

The ages of the eight drowned men varied from 19 to 25. All of them were bachelors except for Ch'angsu Kang, aged 25, who had a wife and children. Because it is believed that people who die in an accident, especially if they are bachelors, may cause their families to suffer misfortunes, a shamanistic ritual for the deceased must be performed whenever a fatal accident occurs.

The *sumangogu-kut* described below was performed by Sok-chul Kim, his wife, and ten members of his own *kut* party. It consisted of 12 rites. The first seance, *hongonjigi-kut* (salvaging or beckoning the drowned spirits) is held at ten in the morning, at sea, where the young fishermen were downed. Five shamans, including one female, carry on a boat eight spirit-poles, offerings and eight bowls, which had been used by the drowned, containing the name plates of the drowned along with paper images of rice and liquor.

They perform the first rite of the *kut* with the families of the drowned men in attendance. After arranging the dishes of food for the dead and lighting candles on the boat, a female shaman bows down in four directions while male shamans play shamanistic music with a *changgo* and gongs. Then the shaman throws into the sea the spirit-bowl tied to the ankle of a living hen (when the dead are women, they use a cock). These are also connected by a cord with the spirit-pole on which they attach the name of the drowned victim written on a piece of paper. The shaman has a member of the family grip the cord in one hand and shake the underwear of the dead in the other hand.

Each of the mothers, sisters, or brothers, shaking the underwear, cries out to the dead to come back. The shaman asks the Dragon King of the sea to return the spirits of the dead, praying, "Dragon King! With your mercy help the dead to return to the road to earth!" After this prayer, a male shaman hauls the bowl and hen into the boat. It is believed that the spirits of the dead stick to the feathers of a hen, which guides them to earth while he calls out the names of the dead, one after another. As the last item of this rite, the shaman throws the offerings wrapped with a piece of white paper into the sea and also pours wine into it. This symbolizes offerings to the Dragon King. Then the participants return to the village from the sea, believing the spirits of the dead come back with them.

The second rite, *yŏngwang-kut* (prayer to Dragon King for the peace of the drowned) is performed after the spirits of the drowned fishermen are transferred to the earth: eight tables for the Dragon

King are set up on the seashore; and with the participation of the family of the deceased, a shaman named Yu-sŏn Kim prays for the Dragon King to bring the young fishermen's spirits back to the earth by dint of his power and to send them away to paradise.

The shaman, performing the 3rd seance, *kolmaegi-kut* (prayer to the guardian deity of village for the peace of the drowned), prays for *Kolmaegi Sonangnim* (the guardian deity of village) to allow the spirits to go to the lotus blossom peak of the Ten Kings in the otherworld. When the *Ch'ŏonwang* (the King of Heaven) pole is brought in after the *ch'ŏngbae-ga* (invocation of spirits song), the family of the deceased tie some money and cloths on the string of the Heaven King's pole. In the meantime the shaman dances and prays, carrying with her a dragon-shaped boat.

Next, the 4th rite, *mŭn-kut* (ritual for passing through the gate of the otherworld) is begun with mortuary tablets, portraits of the drowned persons, and spirit bowls placed on the table for the rite at the gate of village hall. After the *ch'ŏngbae* song is sung, both shamans, a male and a female, playing shamanistic music, come in through the gate from the outside and dance in a circle.

Later rites of the *sumangogu-kut* symbolize the act of opening the gate for the performance of a rite for the deceased spirits. When the *mŭn-kut* is completed, the shamans and the family move the mortuary tablets, the spirit bowls, and the underwear to the altar for a joint rite for the drowned, which is prepared in the village hall. In the altar there is a memorial table decorated with nine kinds of artificial flowers (including lotus flowers which symbolize paradise). On this altar are placed dishes of food offerings, eight spirit-baskets in which paper images of the spirits are put, and eight dragon-shaped ships. (It is believed that the drowned voyage to the otherworld aboard the dragon-shaped ships.)There are also eight rolls of hemp cloth, several *ch'orŏng* (silk-covered lanterns) and several lighted candles in candle holders on the table.

After six in the evening, in front of the altar, the 5th rite, *chomangja-kut* (invocation of the drowned) is performed by a shaman named Soknam Sin. Singing the *ch'ŏngbae* song, the shaman calls out the names of the eight drowned young men. Holding the spirit baskets of each of them and twisting them above the family's head, she moves the family of the drowned to tears by making a statement on behalf of the deceased spirits. Most of the members of the family (more than 200) are women: mothers, wives, and sisters. The sound of their plaintive crying spreads out over the sea. The scene indicates how the various steps of the *kut* are needed to relieve the family members of their grief and suffering.

The next morning, the 6th rite, *palwŏn-kut* (prayer to the gods for the resurrection of the drowned) being completed, the 7th *pangogu-kut* (chamber rite to guide the spirit of the drowned), which is considered the climax of the entire *sumangogu-kut* (shaman ritual for drowned fishermen) begins. A well-known, old, and experienced shaman, Yu-sŏn Kim, takes charge of this rite. The shaman chants the *peridegi* (a variation of *Pari-kongju*) song for three and a half hours.

It should be noted that the *Pari-kongju* song of central Korea is recited monotonously: the shamans merely sit and recite it. *Peridegi*, on the other hand, is a dramatic combination of song, narration, dance, and action, not unlike *P'ansori* (an indigenous theatrical performance). The theme of the *peridegi* is similar to the motif of Parikongju, however. The shaman says, "We perform this *sumangogu-kut* hoping the drowned can enter heaven where they can live long, as in the *Peridegi*. Peridegi gets medicinal water from the otherworld and brings her father back to life."

Here is the last part of the long *Peridegi* shaman song: "You eight spirits are now friends. God bless you! We hope you go to heaven, the best world, not to the hell, not to the bad place. We also hope you bequeath your remaining lives and happiness, which you can't enjoy any more in this world, to your family. We hope again you go to the lotus blossom peak in heaven. *Namu amit'a bul!* (Homage to Amitābha Buddha.)

After finishing the *peridegi* song at two in the afternoon, the shaman builds up eight *yŏngdŭngmalgi* (abodes of the drowned spirits), one for each of the drowned men, and induces the family to hold the spirit baskets and become possessed. For the first three drowned spirits, their mothers hold the spirit baskets. When they become possessed by the spirits of their sons, they don't speak but give answers to the shaman's questions by shaking the spirit baskets.

After the family members sit down with the spirit baskets in their hands, the shaman sits beside them and invokes the spirits by calling out their names. She also chants an incantation while beating a drum. As the shaman keeps beating this drum, the atmosphere around the village hall reaches a climax. One mother who holds a spirit basket becomes possessed with excitement and answers to the shaman's questions by shaking the basket violently. The shaman says, "You came! If you have anything to hope for, tell everything to your family. Are you leaving forever without saying a word? And the bereaved family members calling out the name of the drowned cry out impatiently, "Hello, Chan-su (name of one victim)! Why don't you speak?" In response to these questions, the mother only shakes the basket. When the shaman makes the final statement, that the drowned man can go into the better world by virtue of the *sumangogu-kut,* for which he is indebted to his family, she again shakes the basket up and down in response. The sight touches the family, who, thinking the spirit will go forever to the otherworld, wail for him.

From the family of the fourth victim, Yŏng-dal Cho (aged 23), members of the family, possessed by the spirits, begin to betray the emotions of the dead by speaking. In the case of Yŏng-dal Cho, his father holds the spirit basket first but doesn't become possessed. His mother comes to hold the basket. Holding the basket, she becomes possessed. Shouting "Father was not fair to me!" she beats the father with the spirit basket. (The father had been stern with the drowned man.)The father answers, "I am sorry. But I was stern to you so that you should become a good man." The mother in the place of the dead son says "I went out to sea in order to make a fortune and then the accident occurred!" Then she picks up a guitar from the memorial table since the guitar was a great favorite of the drowned man. She plays the guitar and dances.

The mother of the fifth victim, possessed by his spirit, goes around asking the leading people of the village for travel money for his journey to the otherworld. She takes this money and put it in the spirit basket. She (the spirit) expresses her thanks: "I'm grateful to you all for the *sumangogu-kut.*"

An elder sister of the sixth victim, Yŏng-bok Song, is possessed by her brother's spirit. She says, "My elder sister helped me to go to school with hard-earned money. She had plenty of hardships without parents to support our family. I'm really sorry I can't help her anymore." She finishes her utterances wishing the family every happiness and good luck.

In this way, *taenaerigi* (being possessed by the spirits), which was begun at two in the afternoon, goes on deep into the night in the midst of the weeping of the bereaved families.

The next morning, two more rites, *suri-kut* (exorcizing the evil spirits from the house) and *chioktanil-kut* (prayer to the Ten Kings of the otherworld) are performed in turn.

The 10th rite is *yŏngsanmaji-kut* (shaman rite of cleansing the spirits). The shaman puts the paper images of the spirits on a piece of white paper and scoops them up with an artificial lotus flower. After the shaman puts the images into the spirit bowls, she takes a broom in her right hand and an artificial flower in her left hand. Then she begins to sweep the spirit bowls with the broom drenched in water scented with Chinese juniper, mugwort and pure water. She prays for the drowned men to go to heaven where they will live forever. The act of sweeping the spirit-bowls, in which the paper images are placed, with the broom symbolizes the cleansing of the pollution of death from the drowned. The process is similar to that found in the *sikkim-kut* (shaman rite of bone washing) performed in the southern part of Korea.

As the next item of this rite, the shaman takes the washed spirit images out of the bowls and lays them down on a spirit basket. Dancing with the basket in her hands the shaman sings a song for the drowned. Later the shaman makes a cloth bridge with about twenty meters of white cotton in order to perform the 10th rite. She puts the spirit basket, in which the paper images and mortuary tablets of the spirits are laid, on the bridge and pushes it up to the top side, while singing a *yongson-ga* (a shaman song to make the drowned men get on a dragon-shaped ship and go to the otherworld).

Next is the 11th rite, *kotnori-kut* (celebration with flowers of the resurrection of the drowned spirits). The female shamans pull out the artificial flowers from the memorial table, dance around, and sing a song to the accompaniment of shamanistic music. They finish the *sumangogu-kut* by performing the 12th rite, *sisok-kut* (offering to the miscellaneous spirits). This is the equivalent of the *twijon-gŏri in the chinogwi-kut.*[4]

The third type of trance possession is found in *mugam.* This term designates very vigorous dancing by the client of a *naerim mudang* (possessed or charismatic shaman) during the course of a rite. Here the client puts on the shaman's special costume and dances to the drum. When the governing spirit *(momju)* possesses her, the dancing client begins to jump rapidly up and down to the drum. The *mugam* is a trance dance.[5]

We have till now observed three kinds of trance possession: *Chinogwi-kut, sumangogu-kut,* and *mugam* dancing. A *naerim mudang* becomes a medium of the deceased principally in the seance of *nok-chongbae-gŏri* (the penultimate part of a *chinogwi kut*) and the deceased speaks directly with his family through the mouth of the shaman. It should be noted that this kind of shaman overcomes *sinbyŏng* (possession sickness) during her or his initiation and repeats this experience of healing herself in the process of performing a *chinogwi-kut.* This matches Eliade's statement: "the shaman is not only a sickman; he is, above all, a sickman who has been cured, who has succeeded in curing himself." (Eliade, 1964:27).

A *tan'gol mudang* (hereditary shaman), on the other hand, does not undergo possession sickness when she apprentices herself to the job. Instead, she becomes a shaman by being born into a shaman's family. She can't become a medium of the deceased or possessed by a spirit but helps the family of the dead to be possessed by means of chanting an incantation and beating a drum continuously in the process of *taenaerigi* in the *sumangogu-kut.* As in the case of the shamans of Cheju Island, a *tan'gol mudang* experiences a professional, self-conscious pseudo-possession. However, the hereditary shamans do not have an unexpected, unconscious, genuine-possession, which women of the deceased's family, such as wives, daughters, or daughters-in-law, can undergo.

Many anthropological reports say that shamanistic trance possession occurs most readily among the underprivileged lower classes with repressed social desires (Harris, 1957:1054). Lewis (1981:112-113) similarly notes that possession in ecstatic cults has always attracted followers among the weak and oppressed, and particularly among women in male-dominant societies. In Korea too, possession phenomena take place among the common people, especially among women of the dead man's family. The people of the lower classes, especially poor women, in shamanizing for the dead who meet a violent death, participate themselves in the rite and act as performers—not as an audience—with the shamans. An old Korean proverb says, "Although the mother-in-law wants the shaman to come and dance, she does not like to see her eldest daughter-in-law dance." A severe mother-in-law usually doesn't want to allow her daughters-in-law to take part in *kut* because they can easily enjoy themselves in *mugam* dancing with excitement like a shaman, and the mother-in-law can't prevent them from dancing. This also shows that the daughters-in-law lighten their pent-up feelings of oppression and find solace for themselves with the *kut*. One specialist insists, "Divine possession occurs at the moment when the resentment of the poor and the oppressed are suddenly given vent." (Yŏl-kyu Kim, 1980:63). In the entire process of participation, they, being possessed by the spirit and communicating with the dead, come to believe that the dead man enters heaven and relieve themselves of sorrow.

As can be seen from the above, each type of trance possession in Korean shamanism not only involves role-playing or the assumption of a particular identity, but also has the functions of religious salvation and social-tension reduction in the society.

Endnotes

1. A good deal of research has been devoted to the symptoms of *sinbyŏng*, the possession sickness which is necessary for becoming a *naerim mudang*, a possessed or charismatic shaman. Taegŏn Kim, a specialist in Korean shamanism gives brief accounts of the onset of this initiatory illness and analyzes twenty cases for consistencies in symptoms and precipitating events. He describes the symptoms of the destined shamans as: "persistent illness for no apparent reasons, appetite loss, unwillingness to eat meat and fish, craving for cold water, weakness or pain in the limbs, hallucination, and crazed wanderings." These symptoms can be cured only when the afflicted becomes a shaman through a specific experience of trance state. He notes that "similar experiences mark the would-be shaman in Siberia, the Americas, Africa, and Australia" (Taegŏn Kim, 1970:91-132). In light of this *sinbyŏng* phenomenon, Korean shamans appear to have a close relationship with Siberian shamans and Northern Asian shamans, especially Tungus shamans, in their individual conditions for becoming shamans and recognition and election of a new shaman (Shirokogoroff, 1935:344-351).

On the other hand, Kwang-Il Kim, a psychoanalytically-oriented psychiatrist, divides the *sinbyŏng* syndrome into two phases: a "prodromal phase" and "a depersonalization phase." In the prodromal phase, the destined shaman exhibits, ". . . hysterical or psychosomatic symptoms such as anorexia, weakness, insomnia, indigestion and/or functional paralysis of extremities." In the depersonalization phase, "symptoms are aggravated" and "hallucinatory experiences, dreams of revelation or prophecy, confusion, with/or psychomotor excitement are common additional symptoms." He concludes that "Consequently, '*sinbyŏng*' can be understood not only as a psychopathological manifestation in that they project their longstanding inner conflicts unto the shamanistic complex, but also as a manifestation of unconscious trial for resolving their conflicts by way of projection unto the shamanistic value system." (Kwang-Il Kim, 1972:223-234).

Bou-yŏng Rhi, another psychiatrist but of Jungian orientation, has also done considerable research on Korean shamanism. He agrees that shamans are recovered neurotics or psychotics. Both psychiatrist K.I. Kim (1970, 1972, and 1974) and B.Y. Rhi (1968 and 1970) have reached these similar conclusions from their independent studies and perceived Korean shamanism as an institutionalized system of sublimation, which has both positive and negative effects.

Since W.G. Bogoras and M.A. Czaplicka, in the early second decade of 20th century, to A. Ohlmarks, the last investigator who favors explaining shamanism by arctic hysteria, Siberian shamanism has been studied especially as a psychopatholoqical phenomenon. Recently Devereux (1956:23 and 1961) "characterizes the shaman as a severe neurotic or psychotic who serves his society as a deputy lunatic" (cited here from Harvey 1979:242).

S.M. Shirokogoroff expressed the opinion that a shaman has a normal personality (1923:248-249). And U. Harva seconds his point in noting that though there is no satisfactory explanation of symptoms of possession sickness, well-reputed Siberian shamans must not be considered as only mad lunatics (1971, Japanese edition:411). H. Findeisen says that possession sickness which a novice must undergo in order to become a shaman is generally believed to be an uneasiness or mental affliction. Nobody can explain the true mental disorder of the kind, but as soon as the shaman, selected by the spirits, holds a shaman drum-stick, he is believed to be free from the sickness forever, and he never suffers from the sickness again (1957:51).

In relation to the opinions of these researchers on shamanism, the Korean folk-view of shamansim can be summed up as follows: (1) the experience of disorder of some form is an essential feature in the recruitment of a shaman; (2) afflictions alone do not automatically make a shaman of the victim—they must be overcome; and (3) the relationship between a shaman and possessing spirits are transactional and mutually bonding, as in a marriage (Harvey, 1979:251).

2. K. Harvey outlines the personal attributes of a *naerim mudang* after completing a good study of this type of shaman: (1) a high level of intelligence; (2) above average capacity for creative improvisation (they were imaginative and capable of improvising verbally, behaviorally, and in the use of available resources); (3) above average verbal fluency and persuasiveness; (4) strong goal orientation (they tended to be willful, self-centered, self-reliant, and self-directed); (5) keen sensitivity to intuitive cues of others; (6) calculating and manipulative interpersonal skills which enabled them to manage social situations strategically; (7) a sharp sense of justice in terms of their own standards; and (8) an above-average repertoire of aptitudinal and/or achieved dramatic and artistic attributes such as singing and dancing (Harvey, 1979:235-236).

3. Other research has found that the Goldi tribe or Tungus tribe in Siberia express both the road of spirits and the road of the shaman by using a cord, string, or rope. (U. Harva, 1938:passim).

4. "After the shamanizing, when the members of the audience recollect the various moments of the performance, their great psychophysiological emotion and the hallucinations of sight and hearing, they have a deep satisfaction, greater than that from the emotion produced by theatrical and musical performances, literature and general artistic phenomena of the European complex, because in shamanizing the audience consists at the same time of actors and participants." (Shirokogoroff, 1935:331).

5. The following is a comparison of ritual and theatre made by Schechner (1977:75).

EFFICACY (Ritual)	ENTERTAINMENT (Theatre)
results	fun
link to an absent Other	only for those here
abolishes time, symbolic time	emphasizes now
brings Other here	audience is the Other
performer possessed, in trance	performer know what he's doing
audience participates	audience watches
audience believes	audience appreciates
criticism is forbidden	criticism is encouraged
collective creativity	individual creativity

Bibliography

Akiba, Takashi, 1950, *A Field Study of Shamanism in Korea.* Nara, Japan: Yotokusha, (in Japanese).

Choe, Kil-song, 1982, *Community Ritual and Social Structure in Village Korea.* Asian Folklore Studies 41:39-48.

Crapanzano, Vincent & Garrison, Vivian, 1977, *Case Studies in Spirit Possession.* New York: John Wiley & Sons.

Czaplicka, M.A., 1914, *Aboriginal Siberia: A Study in Social Anthropology.* Oxford: At the Clarendon Press.

Eliade, Mircea, 1964, *Shamanism: Archaic Techniques of Ecstasy.* New York: Bollingen Foundation.

Findeisen, Hans, 1957, *Schamanentum.* Zurich: Europa Verlag. (1977, Japanese edition)

Nioradze, Georg, 1925, *Der Schamanismus bei den Siberischen Volkern.* Stuttgart. (1946, Korean Edition).

Goodman, Felicitas D. & Others, 1974, *Trance, Healing and Hallucination.* New York: John Wiley & Sons.

Harris, Grace, 1957, Possession "Hysteria" in a Kenya Tribe. *American Anthropologist* 59: 1046-1066.

Harva, Uno, 1938, *Religiosen Vorstelungen der Altaischen Volker.* Helsinki (1971, Japanese edition)

Harvey, Youngsook Kim, 1979, *Six Korean Women: The Socialization of Shamans.* St. Paul: West Publishing Co.

Kendall, Laurel M., 1977, Mugam: The Dance in Shaman's Clothing. *Korean Journal* 17 (12): 38-44.

———, 1979, *Restless Spirits: Shaman and Housewife in Korean Ritual Life.* Ph.D. dissertation, Columbia University.

Kim, Kwang-Il, 1972, Sin-Byung: a Culture-bound depersonaliza-tion Syndrome Neuropsychiatry. Neuropsychiatry 11(4): 223-234. (In Korean with title and abstract in English).

Kim T'aegon, 1970, A Study of Shaman's Mystic Illness during Initiation Process in Korea. *Journal of Asian Women.* 9:91-132. (In Korean, with English Summary).

———, 1982, *A Study of Korean Shamanism.* Seoul: Jibmun-dang. (In Korean, with abstract in English).

Kim, Yŏl-kyu, 1980, Several forms of Korean Folk Rituals, Including Shaman Rituals. In "Customs and Manners in Korea." Shin-Yong Chun, gen.ed. Seoul: International Cultural Foundation.

Kirby, Ernest Theodore, 1975. *Ur-Drama: The Origins of Theatre.* New York: New York University Press.

Rhi, Bou-Yong, 1970, Analytic-Psychological Study on Shamanistic Treatment of the Dead Spirit in Korean Shamanism. *The New Medical Journal* 13(1): 79-94 (in Korean, with abstract in German).

Lewis, L.M., 1971, *Ecstatic Religion: An Anthropological Study of Spirit Possession and Shamanism.* Middlesex, England: Penguin Books.

Schechner, Richard, 1977, *Essays on Performance Theory 1970-1976.* New York: Darma Book Specialists.

Shirokogoroff, S.M., 1923, General Theory of Shamanism among the Tungus". *Journal of the Royal Asiatic Society,* North China Branch 54:248-249.

———, 1935, *Psychomental Complex of The Tungus.* London: Kegan Paul, Trench, Trubner & Co.

Glossary of Shamanistic Terms

Buju sin
God of Fodder

Ch'a cha'a ung
Early Silla name for ruler, having the meanings of shaman or family elder

Chae-ung
Doll-like image used in ritual, receives the evil spirits and is destroyed

Chagŭn-kut
The "Lesser" exorcism. see Kŭn-kut

Chesŏk halmang
Buddhist deity Śakra; fertility goddess on Cheju Island

Chinogwi-kut
A ritual to appease angry spirits of the dead ancestors

Cho-wang
God of the kitchen and sacred fire; also called the God of Women

Ch'o yong
Shrine for the spirits of ancestors

Chŏm
Divination related to illness

Chosang-gŏri
Seance ritual for contact with ancestors

Chungdi garŭm-gŏri
Ritual of "Divided Cloth Bridge" by which the dead are assisted in their journey

Gŏri
Seance ritual for contact with the dead (see p. 163 for a list of the many types)

Hongonjigi-kut
Ritual for assisting the spirits of those who have drowned

Hwa-jŏn
Fire ritual/dance for exorcism of evil spirits

Iret-tang
"Seventh Day" shrine for rituals on the 7th and 27th of each month

Je-suk sin
God identified in ritual with rice

Kang sin
Name given to shaman who is possessed by gods

Kang sin ch'e hŏm
The experience of the descent of the spirit into the Mudang. see sinbyŏng ch'e-hŏm

Kang sin ja
The person possessed by the gods

Kilkkal chugi
Ritual of "Preparing the Road," symbolic for sending away the god of the ritual.

Kŏngsu
Message given during the ritual by the gods explaining the cause of illness

Kunung-sin
God associated with beans in the ritual

Kŭn-kut
The "great Exorcism" similar to P'algwan

Kut
Shaman ceremony, often related to exorcism of evil spirits

Mudang
Female shaman

Mugam
Group dance during shaman ceremony

Mugyehon
Marriage between two hereditary shaman families

Myŏng-du
Spirit of female child that possesses Shaman. see Tongja

Myŏng-du
Ritual mirror of Shaman

Myŏnggam
Messenger of the Other World

Naerim Kut
The ritual for enshrining the god in the body of the shaman

Ogari-sin
God of "Pots and Pans". Related to household shrine

Ŏp
God of fortune. see T'ŏ-ju

O-sin
Ritual for amusing the god during ritual. see gŏri

Paksu
Male Shaman

P'algwan
Ritual in honor of the Celestial King and the Five Famous Mountains and Rivers

Pang'ul
Ritual bell. see Sammyŏngdu

Pansu
   Male shaman

Pison
   Shaman rituals performed by those who have no knowledge of
   song or dance elements

P'oje dan
   Shrine where men perform New Year's rituals

Ponhyang
   Village Shrine

Ponp'uri
   Shaman epic

Puchaeng sin
   God associated with ashes during ritual

P'udakkŭri
   Ritual for general healing

Pyŏng Kut
   Ritual for healing major illness

Sajegwŏn
   Priestly authority of shaman

Salp'uri
   Ritual for healing acute illness

Sammyŏngdu
   The three tools of the shaman: sword, bell, and divining rod

Samp'an
   Divining rod. see Sammyŏngdu

San sin
   God associated with sesame seeds during ritual

Segyŏng
   Fertility goddess

Simbang
> Name for shamans on Cheju Island; also priest of a shrine usually involved in divination

Sinkhal
> The sword of the god of the ritual. see Sammyŏngdu

Sinbyŏng ch'e-hŏm
> The experience of mystic illness in the process of becoming a shaman

Sŏn Mudang
> Shamans named after the gods who possess them

Sŏng-ju
> God of the Household

Sŏngmu Kwajŏng
> The process of becoming a shaman. see Sinbyŏng Ch'ehŏm

Song-sin
> Ritual for sending away the god during ritual; also a type of placation of spirits. see gŏri

Sonbibim
> Prayer offered by Mudang for the sick

Sŏngmu ŭi Sik
> Ritual associated with becoming a shaman

Sunang sin
> God associated with the red beans during ritual

Suri Kut
> Exorcism of evil spirits from the house

Taegam-gŏri
> Seance for "High" government officials called on to aid with problems

Tan'gol p'an
> Shaman who inherits priestly authority through the family

Toggyong
> Ritual reading of Buddhist and Taoist scripture

T'ŏju
> God of the residence lot, often called God of the Backyard

T'ŏjut Taegam
> God of the House

Tongja
> Spirit of Male Child that possesses shaman during seance. see myŏngdu

Tuhaju sin
> God associated with buckwheat during ritual

Yŏdŭret-tang
> "Eighth Day" Shrine for rituals on 8th, 18th, and 28th day of the month; also associated with snake shrines

Yŏngdong
> Ritual dedicated to the Buddha

Yŏngdŭng Kut
> Ritual for the Spirit of the Wind

Yŏnggam
> A demon of the ocean; also God of the Smith

Yŏng sin
> God associated with water during ritual

Yŏng sil
> Ritual for calling the god to the ritual. see gŏri.

Index